BRIGHT NOTES

THE COLOR PURPLE AND OTHER WORKS BY ALICE WALKER

Intelligent Education

Nashville, Tennessee

BRIGHT NOTES: The Color Purple and Other Works
www.BrightNotes.com

No part of this publication may be used or reproduced in any manner whatsoever without written permission, except in the case of brief quotations in critical articles and reviews. For permissions, contact Influence Publishers http://www.influencepublishers.com.

ISBN: 978-1-645420-16-3 (Paperback)
ISBN: 978-1-645420-17-0 (eBook)

Published in accordance with the U.S. Copyright Office Orphan Works and Mass Digitization report of the register of copyrights, June 2015.

Originally published by Monarch Press.
Barbara Christian
2020 Edition published by Influence Publishers.

Interior design by Lapiz Digital Services. Cover Design by Thinkpen Designs.

Printed in the United States of America.

Library of Congress Cataloging-in-Publication Data forthcoming.
Names: Intelligent Education
Title: BRIGHT NOTES: The Color Purple and Other Works
Subject: STU004000 STUDY AIDS / Book Notes

CONTENTS

1)	Introduction to Alice Walker	1
2)	Plot Analysis	27
3)	Character Analysis	47
4)	Critical Commentary	66
5)	Critics Respond to the Novel the Color Purple	80
6)	Critics Respond to the Film Version of the Color Purple	93
7)	The Third Life of Grange Copeland	105
8)	In Love & Trouble: Stories of Black Women	109
9)	Revolutionary Petunias and Other Poems	112
10)	Meridian	115
11)	Good Night Willie Lee, I'll see you in the morning	119
12)	You can't keep a good woman down	121

13)	Once	124
14)	Walker after the Color Purple	126
15)	Ideas for Papers, Discussions, and Oral Reports	129
16)	Bibliography	138

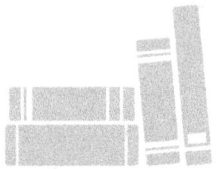

INTRODUCTION TO ALICE WALKER

ALICE WALKER'S LIFE, WORKS, AND PHILOSOPHICAL CONCERNS

A world-famous writer. In 1983 Alice Walker's novel *The Color Purple* won her the Pulitzer Prize. She is the first African-American woman writer to win that award. *The Color Purple* has since made her internationally famous. But Walker had been publishing books since 1968. To date, she has developed her vision and craft in four volumes of poetry, a children's story, two collections of short stories, many essays, and three novels. *The Color Purple* is part of a larger body of work that is characterized by Walker's commitment to the "survival whole" of black people; to the legacy of black women's creative forms, as well as their struggle to become free; and to an exploration of the black South's history and traditions.

CHILDHOOD INFLUENCES

It is no accident that Walker's work emphasizes these three elements. She was born on February 9, 1944, in Eatonton, Georgia, the eighth and last child of Willie Lee and Minnie Lou Grant Walker. Her parents were sharecroppers, which meant that they farmed for a pittance of land owned by a white "boss man" who controlled practically every aspect of their livelihood- from the shacks they were forced to live in to the yield from their crops. From a very young age, Walker experienced the racism of the South and its restrictions on black people's development. Despite long years of toil, her father was hardly able to feed and clothe his family. While raising eight children, her mother made everything her family wore, and worked hard in the fields, as well as in white women's kitchens. Walker's childhood was filled with stories of past lynchings and, like other Southern black children, she had to address her little white girlfriends "Miss." Her first novel, *The Third Life of Grange Copeland*, which traces three generations of a sharecropping family, and many of her poems in *Once and Revolutionary Poems* are based on memories of her childhood.

AN OUTCAST AND HER NOTEBOOK

A traumatic accident occurred when she was eight. She lost sight of one eye when one of her older brothers shot her with a BB gun. For years, an ugly scar covered her eye and it was feared that she would lose the other eye. As a result of her injury, Walker felt like an outcast. Her sense of her difference certainly contributed to her ability to ask questions that others did not. She kept a notebook in which she began to look closely at relationships and to write poems. Ironically, Walker received a "rehabilitation scholarship" from Georgia, a state known for its racism. Along with her achievement as valedictorian of her class, that scholarship made it possible for her to go to Spelman, a college for black women in Atlanta, Georgia.

During her childhood, Walker also experienced another important quality of black Southern life - that of community and struggle. Her father was the first black man to vote in Putman County, despite death threats. Black families bonded together to build schools for their children. Unlike blacks in the North, no black person feared another black, not even the convicts on the chain gangs, which were still a part of Southern life. Walker has said in one of her essays that "what the black Southern writer inherits as a natural right is a sense of community."

"IN SEARCH OF OUR MOTHERS' GARDENS"

Perhaps for her the most important person of that community was her mother. Walker has said that many of her own written stories are based on stories her mother told her and that she absorbed not only the stories themselves but also the urgency with which her mother told them. Just as important, her mother gave the young Walker the legacy of understanding that beauty is necessary to life. Despite her long days, Minnie Lou Walker woke early to plant gardens that became famous throughout the county. She transformed, with the little she had, the shacks, in which the family lived, into homes. In her classic essay, "In Search of Our Mother's Gardens," Walker tells us the effect her mother's art had on her:

I notice that it is only when my mother is working in her flowers that she is radiant, almost to be point of being invisible-except as Creator: hand and eye. She is involved in work that her soul must have.

    Years later, Walker developed literary forms based on the legacy of black women's creativity in the only media they were allowed in Southern society-quilting, gardening, cooking, storytelling.

WALKER AND HISTORY

Walker also grew up in a family well-versed in its own history, a factor that may have encouraged the importance of history in all of her work. It may also be why her three novels depict generations of a Southern black family. She knew, for example, about her, great-great-great-great-grandmother Mary Poole who, after Emancipation, walked with two babies on her hip from Virginia to Eatonton, where she established their family. It is in honor of this ancestor that Alice retains her maiden name, Walker. She also heard stories about her grandfather and grandmother. In the early 1970s walker wrote the poem "Burial" to her grandmother, Rachel, whose husband did not even notice that her name was misspelled on her tombstone. Later, Walker gave new life to Rachel and her husband; they are the bases of her characters Celie and Mister in *The Color Purple*.

When she left Eatonton, Georgia, the seventeen-year-old Walker went to school first at Spelman College in Georgia, then two years later, to Sarah Lawrence College in New York. During her junior year she went, as an exchange student, to Africa. Her experiences in these three places had a profound effect on her work.

EFFECTS OF CIVIL RIGHTS MOVEMENT ON WALKER

Walker went to Spelman College in the early 1960s when the Civil Rights Movement, what she calls "the Southern Revolution," was having a transformative effect on the nation. She reports in one of her essays on the Civil Rights Movement that the face of Martin Luther King, Jr., was one of the first she saw on the television set that her family was finally able to afford. In Atlanta, she met young leaders of the movement, e.g., John Lewis and Ruby Doris Robinson, and she participated in demonstrations where "everyone was conquering fear by holding the hands of the person next to them." Her experiences there are one source for many of her poems in *Once* (1968), her first collection of poems, *Revolutionary Petunias* (1973), her second collection of poetry, and for *Meridian* (1976), her novel about the Civil Rights Movement.

Walker was deeply aware that the movement helped make it possible for young Southern blacks like herself to envision actually following paths to which her parents, even her older brothers and sisters, had no access. She makes this clear by ending her first novel, *The Third Life of Grange Copeland* (1970), with the arrival of Civil Rights workers to the racist town in which Ruth, her young **protagonist**, lives, an indication that there is hope she might "survive whole." The Civil Rights Movement is a definitive factor in Walker's life and helped to open avenues which made it possible for her to become a writer.

The Civil Rights Movement of the 1950s and the 1960s was a people's movement that attempted, through nonviolent means, such as demonstrations and boycotts, to eradicate the segregationist and racist laws of this country. Its philosophy was similar to that of the great Indian leader, M. Gandhi's belief that violence violates all life and is inherently evil. Walker also characterizes the movement's philosophy as Animism, an African philosophical position that she defines as the belief that "Spirit inhabits all life." For her that belief is rooted, as well, in Southern black culture, from the spirituals and slave narratives to the rituals of the black church.

VIOLENCE AND SOCIAL CHANGE

Walker's participation in and observation of the Civil Rights Movement deepened her sense of how violence is a predominant thread in the American social fabric and affected her intense exploration of societal violence in all her work. Her novel *The Third Life of Grange Copeland* dramatically demonstrates the effects of racism, a societal system of violence, on three generations of a black sharecropping family and how societal violence results in family and personal violence. Her novel Meridian explores the question of whether violence is necessary to social change, a question that must be confronted by all serious revolutionary movements. And her novel *The Color Purple* depicts the violence men inflict on women in order to feel powerful in their families and in the general society.

In all three novels, violence is transcended through the major character's growing awareness of the meaning of life, of how spirit inhabits all life, and of how the violation of any living thing affects all other living things. Walker uses Nature, trees, flowers, rocks as an embodiment of her philosophy. For example, the most glorious tree in the county, the Sojourner Tree in Meridian, which embodies their history, is cut down by Saxon College students during a demonstration; but by the end of the novel, when Meridian has transformed herself, it begins to sprout. The Civil Rights Movement is not only a source of Walker's concern with societal violence, it is also an influence on her philosophy about the oneness of all life.

EFFECTS OF WOMEN'S MOVEMENT ON WALKER

The Sojourner Tree in Meridian was inspired by the beautiful cherry trees at Spelman. Walker also used this college to explore another **theme** in her work-a celebration of black women's history and her protest of sexism, which affects all women. Spelman had traditionally been a school noted for its espousal of black middle-class values, a place where "being a lady" was paramount. In her essay, "Lulls: A Return to the South," Walker tells us about some of the women she'd experienced in her childhood, women who "did everything," who could hunt and fish and who also dressed beautifully. But such women would not have been considered ladies at Spelman. Walker uses Spelman as the basis for Saxon College in her novel Meridian, and as a means of protesting the concept of ladyhood that restricted even black women's ability to struggle for the freedom of the race.

Nonetheless, Spelman was an important institution for the preservation of the history of black women. Walker was later to use its archives as the basis of the Nettie sections in *The Color Purple*. For generations, Spelman graduates had done outrageous things, such as going to Africa as missionaries and helping to galvanize social black Southern movements. The school itself represented the two major influences on black women that dominate Walker's works: the tradition of black women's history and the restrictions that have affected them even in black society.

MALE CHAUVINISM IN AFRICA

After spending two years at Spelman, the young Walker transferred to Sarah Lawrence College in New York, and during her junior year traveled to Africa as an exchange student. While black nationalists of the period were evoking romantic images of Africa, she experienced it firsthand. Her sojourn there was the impetus for some of the poems in *Once*, as well as for the African sections in *The Color Purple*. Of black women in Africa, Walker was later to say, "we are the mules there as well as here."

Her trip to Africa also resulted in another significant event in her life. When she returned to Sarah Lawrence College, the twenty-year-old Walker discovered she was pregnant. At that time, abortion was illegal, but she knew that her pregnancy would halt her education and shame her parents. While her friends looked for an abortionist, she discovered how "alone woman was in her body." Convinced that she would commit suicide, she urgently wrote poems and stuffed them in the box of Muriel Rukeyser, her teacher at Sarah Lawrence and one of America's foremost women poets. These poems would become *Once*, her first published volume.

RACISM AND SEXISM....

What Walker intensely felt, as the result of her pregnancy and abortion, was the impact of the double standard that existed for men and women in the society. She realized how necessary it was for women, as women, to achieve their freedom. The young Walker became one of the first contemporary African-American women writers to overtly explore sexism in black society in her first novel, *The Third Life of Grange Copeland*, and in her controversial first collection of short stories, In *Love & Trouble*, as well as to demonstrate how the interaction of sexism and racism results in grave restrictions on black women's lives.

Walker, as well, has been an active participant in the Women's Movement. She knew that one cause of the second wave of American feminism, which erupted in the early 1970s, was the Civil Rights Movement in much the same way that the Women's Rights Movement of the nineteenth century had evolved out of the Abolitionist Movement. White women activists of both these black movements had discovered the extent to which they were restricted as women. Black women also experienced sexism within the Civil Rights Movement, which was necessarily affected by gender definitions of the entire society. Like Meridian in Walker's novel, most women were initially perceived as typists rather than as potential leaders. And even when they obviously had been leaders, their activities were subordinated to male leaders, just as prominent black women activists, like the nineteenth-century feminist Ida B. Wells, had been ignored in black history books. Such was the case with Rosa Parks, who had refused to give up her seat to a white man, an act that precipitated the Montgomery Bus Boycott in 1955 and is generally identified as the beginning of the Modern Civil Rights Movement. Although Mrs. Parks had been an activist for many years, her act was preempted by the nation's focus on Martin Luther King, Jr., the young preacher who was drafted by Montgomery's black leaders to become the boycott's spokesman. Limited by their media visibility, women in the Civil Rights Movement learned much about political tactics and eventually used these lessons to analyze and confront the sexism and racism in the society.

.... ARE INTERACTIVE CONCEPTS

Then as now, the Women's Movement is often perceived as a white Women's Movement. Black women are often categorized solely as "black" as if they were not women as well, an attitude that is clear in the phrase "women and minorities." Walker protested such a characterization of black women. In her essay, "One Child of One's Own" (1979), she addresses the racism of white feminists and the refusal of blacks to address sexism in a discussion that summarizes her protests of that decade. She answers the question as to whether for black women, sex should come before race, or race before sex, by pointing out the obvious fact that black people come in both sexes. She traces the history of American feminism and reminds us that black women like Sojourner Truth and Ida B. Wells were at the forefront of the nineteenth-century Women's Rights Movement. And she also emphasizes that the Women's Movement refers to women moving all over the world. Walker comments: "To the extent that black women dissociate themselves from the Women's Movement they abandon their responsibilities to women throughout the world." Through her work, Walker has challenged the idea that sexism and racism are separate categories. For black women, they are interactive concepts, and unless black women challenge them both, they will not achieve their freedom.

The two political movements that evolved during Walker's youth - the Civil Rights Movement and the Women's Movement- are crucial to the directions she has taken in her work. The subjects she has explored, from the restrictive ideology of motherhood to the history of black women's creativity, are set in the spaces these movements opened for her.

WALKER AND THE AFRICAN-AMERICAN LITERARY TRADITION

Walker studied literature while she was in college. Like most writers, she has been influenced in her work by writers that preceded her. She tell us, in an early interview, that she loved Russian writers like Tolstoy and Gorky because of their ability to create individual characters within the context of a complex society. She is drawn to women writers like the Brontes and Doris Lessing because "their characters can always envision a solution, an evolution to higher consciousness on the part of the society, even when society itself cannot." She has been influenced by the German writers Hermann Hesse and Rainer Maria Rilke in her work because they ask the unaskable. She is deeply influenced by Native American writer Black Elk, African writer Elechi Amadi, and Latin American writer Gabriel Garcia

Marquez, because they seem "like musicians, at one with their cultures and their historical subconscious."

USE OF AFRICAN-AMERICAN WRITERS

Although she was exposed in school to writers from different parts of the world, neither the black school, Spelman, or the white school, Sarah Lawrence, introduced her to African-American writers. The only writer she learned about in school who included African-Americans in his work was William Faulkner, whose character Dilsey, in *The Sound and Fury*, Walker calls "an embarrassment to black people." Her concern with this blatant omission in education would result in her writing a biography for children of the great black writer, Langston Hughes (1974), and many essays on African-American writers such as "The Divided Life of Jean Toomer" (1980). She included African-American writers in her work, for instance, Richard Wright in her short story, "A Sudden Trip Home in the Spring" (1981), as well as historical figures such as Ida B. Wells in "Advancing Luna" (1981). She has even used contemporary African-American women writers directly in her work, e.g., June Jordan in her poems, Audre Lorde in the short story, "Coming Apart" (1981). Perhaps the most important explorations of the black female literary tradition are her two essays, "In Search of Our Mothers' Gardens" (1974) and "Looking for Zora" (1975).

In "In Search of Our Mothers' Gardens," Walker looks closely at eighteenth-century African-American women writer Phyllis Wheatley, who was the first black and the second female to be acknowledged as a poet in America. Her work had been denigrated by twentieth-century blacks, who considered it the work of a colonized mind. But for Walker, this literary maternal ancestor of hers exemplified the contradictions of being a black writer in America. Phyllis was a slave and torn by "contrary instincts." "Her loyalties were completely divided as was, without question, her mind," and yet she preserved "the notion of song." For Walker, the black women writers that followed Phyllis, writers like Nella Larsen and even the intrepid Zora Neale Hurston, were hindered by "contrary instincts," as they tried to be writers in a society that denied them, as black women, any such capacity.

In analyzing the literary tradition of African-American women writers of the nineteenth and early twentieth century, Walker is able to see how important it is to bear in mind those forms that allowed black women more freedom to express themselves, folk forms such as the blues, quilting, gardening.

WALKER RESCUES ZORA HURSTON

In "Looking for Zora," Walker does more than analyze a literary tradition, she plays a critical role in the rescue of this great Southern black woman writer from oblivion. Walker had never heard of this literary ancestor of hers-a black woman like her, a Southerner like her-until she was working on a story "The Revenge of Hannah Kemhuff" in the early 1970s. In her library search, Walker found the name of Zora Neale Hurston in a footnote. Walker finally located the curse she needed for her story, which she used as well in an essay, "Only Justice can Stop a Curse" (1982).

More important, that footnote led her to Hurston's great novel, *Their Eyes Were Watching God* (1936), which inspired the young Walker to find out everything she could about her literary ancestor. She realized that Hurston had been neglected not because of her work but because she was judged by her life. Walker commented that "since black women writers are not, it would seem, very likeable - until recently they were the least willing worshippers of male supremacy - comments about them tend to be cruel." Hurston had been a "bodacious" woman, one who refused to fit the image of the proper black woman. Walker understood how much the judgment on Hurston could happen to Walker as well.

By the time she'd discovered Zora, Walker had published *The Third Life of Grange Copeland*. Rather than focusing on her work, critics had commented on her "life-style," that she had recently married a white Civil Rights lawyer, Mel Levanthal. Walker responded by pointing out how many black male writers, like Richard Wright and Leroi Jones, whom these critics admired, had themselves been interracially married. She knew that black women, because they were women, were not allowed such prerogatives. In searching for Zora, she insisted that black women writers be judged by their work. Her example would help to give rise to a whole body of black feminist criticism. In helping to get Hurston's work republished and in putting a tombstone on her unmarked grave, Walker was not only giving us back a great writer, she was insisting that contemporary African-American women take responsibility for sustaining their writers. No doubt, her decision to develop her own publishing company, Wild Trees Press, which she did in 1984, is due partly to her sense of the precariousness of that history. It is one of the first presses in America to be owned and run by a black woman.

WALKER'S THEMES AND TECHNIQUES

Quilting as a Theme and a Technique

After finishing college, Walker lived for a short time in New York, then returned to the South. From the mid 1960s to the mid 1970s, she lived in Tougaloo, Mississippi, during which time she had a daughter, Rebecca, in 1969. In Mississippi, she taught in Freedom Schools, collected oral histories and folklore from black women, and paid particular attention to their storytelling. She would, during this period, publish her first and second volumes of poetry; her first novel; her first collection of short stories as well as many essays, particularly "In Search of Our Mothers' Gardens" (1974) and "In Search of Zora Neale Hurston" (1975). Her work from this period is characterized by her search for forms that best express the spirit of African-American women's history and culture. It was also during this time that she developed a literary technique based on quilting.

During the early 1970s, Alice Walker published a short story "Everyday Use," and an essay, "In Search of Our Mothers' Gardens," which explored the creative legacy of Southern black women, and used quilting as a powerful symbol of that legacy. The process of quilting highlights important aspects of Walker's concept of art and of the structuring of her novels.

Smithsonian quilt: a work of art

In "In Search of Our Mothers' Gardens," Walker asks the question, How did the creative spirit of the Southern black woman survive and flourish, despite the brutality of her history? She gives us a description of a quilt created by an "anonymous black woman in Alabama, 100 years ago," which now hangs in the Smithsonian Institute as a priceless work of art. For Walker, this black woman, and others like her who perfected art through gardening, cooking, and quilting, are the black women artists of the past who had no access to the pen, to the canvas, or to clay. Instead of looking only to "high" art, contemporary, black women artists also needed to look to "low media" for models upon which to base their art.

In her short story "Everyday Use" Walker explores even further the theme of the quilt as one significant medium through which black women were allowed to express their creativity. Walker emphasizes the significance of the quilt by contrasting two sisters: the seemingly ignorant Maggie who has not gone to school, but knows how to quilt, and the educated, fashionable Wangero who assesses quilts primarily as works of art to enhance her own value. Their mother tells this story and ends her contrast of the two sisters' characters by snatching the quilts away from the selfish Wangero, who does not care about her family, and giving them to Maggie, who loves her people and makes quilts from their worn clothes.

Waste transformed into beauty

In both these pieces, Walker stresses that the quilt is a work of functional beauty created from bits and pieces that are seen as worthless. For Walker, the creative legacy of the Southern black woman has been her ability to create much out of little and to use her imagination to transform waste into beauty.

Quilts are made for everyday use; they warm the body and nurture the spirit with beauty and the memory of those who wore the scraps from which they are made. All Walker novels are based on quilting, the imaginative use of short units that may at first seem incongruous, to create a beautiful and meaningful whole. Moreover, her novels are, like quilts, created for everyday use. They address concrete issues of "survival whole" and fulfillment with segments of the history of "ordinary" African-American women.

Walker's first novel, *The Third Life of Grange Copeland*, consists of motifs of Grange Copeland's first life: grinding poverty, toil, powerlessness, in the face of the white boss man who turns him to stone. These, in turn, result in his drunken bouts, the beating of his wife Margaret, and the exploitation of the local whore Josie, the neglect of his son Brownfield, and finally his desertion of his family to escape, like a runaway slave, to the North. In spite of his attempts to improve his life by marrying Mem, a schoolteacher, Brownfield repeats the same pattern in his life, until he murders his wife on a Christmas Eve. Walker arranges the motifs of this quilt so that we see how societal racism affects this family. But the pattern of this quilt begins to change when Grange returns home, disillusioned, from his second life in the North. He commits himself to helping his granddaughter Ruth to survive by teaching her about the land and about the history and culture of their family. Still, he has created Brownfield, the son who destroys his father by enlisting the judicial system of the South to reclaim Ruth. Although Grange is murdered by the police at the end of the novel, Civil Rights workers are entering the town as Walker asserts the new pattern that Grange has created.

A crazy quilt

In *Meridian*, her second novel, Walker improvises more freely, in the creation of a crazy quilt. She juxtaposes the respective histories of Southern blacks and Native Americans, the motifs of violence throughout American history as well as the decade of the 1960s and the life of Meridian, an "ordinary lower middle-class Southern woman" to create a quilt of change that at first seems incoherent. By choosing representative aspects of growing up, such as the need to have a boyfriend and yet remain a virgin, with examples of our national collective history, such as the nation's television viewing of John Kennedy's funeral, and the history of black children whose lives are precariously poised even before they are born, Walker creates for us a quilt of the Civil Rights Movement and the questions it posed. One essential motif is that of motherhood, of the nurturing of life, which is, for her, basic to revolutionary change.

Quilting in The Color Purple

Walker changes the pattern of quilting in *The Color Purple* to emphasize the history and culture of women. Consisting entirely of letters, a short unit and one which feminist historians have found to be an important source of women's history, as well as charting her novel as a slave narrative, a basic form in black literature, Walker creates a womanist form-a quilt of sisterhood. In the novel, Celie is creating a quilt called "Sister's Choice," Walker's comment on her own process. And the novel itself is based on motifs of three's, the most obvious being the pattern of letters, from Celie to God, then from Nettie to Celie, and finally from Celie to Nettie, as Walker uses the form of the novel to dramatize the basic motif of sisterhood.

Walker and Romare Bearden

Walker's technique of quilting combines philosophical and aesthetic views of traditional and modern cultures. The quilts that African-American women created in the New World are based on African concepts of the connected nonlinear quality of life, evident in traditional Dahomeyan quilts that combine motifs of apparently disjointed events to create a visual pattern of history. Modern African-American painters, such as Romare Bearden, a painter whom Walker admires, have used the technique of juxtaposing apparently contradictory units to exemplify African-American history and culture. His work appeared on the hardcover edition of *Meridian*. Juxtaposing short units allows the modern artist to use her imagination in an efficient way to create new works of art from apparently familiar and cliched stories which modern readers can experience in short intervals, an important quality in this over-stimulated and extremely busy world. Walker's technique of quilting, then, is based on the traditional and yet is modernist its style.

The Importance of History in Walker's Work

Walker's emphasis on quilting as a **theme** and technique is related to the importance of history in her work, for quilting is a folk art that preserves the memory of those who have gone before us. Often people conceive of history only in terms of governments, rulers, and battles of the past. For Walker, history refers to the collective experience of everyday folk, their relationships with each other, with the young to the old, with women to men, which are often embodied in their family structure, rituals, mores, music, language. For her, as for many African-American writers, literature is one means of recording the history of black folk, particularly of women, a subject usually omitted from the official history.

Even when blacks are included in history books, they are often treated only in terms of their leaders and in relation to whites, the dominant group in the United States. Walker has said that she writes, not only to tell a story but to record as well the history of her people, Southern blacks, and most specifically her own family. Because her family history intersects with the history of other Southern blacks, who were slaves and then freedmen who were dispossessed of their land, she, of necessity, focuses on the collective experience of an entire group.

Change: her major theme

This concern with history permeates all of Walker's work, her poems, short stories, essays, and novels. Her three novels use the generations of a family to show the process of personal and societal change, the major **theme** of her work. In an early interview the young Walker says that anything of the immediate present is too superficial; one needs historical perspectives to give depth and resonance to a work of art. She concretizes that perception in a talk in the early 1970s with critic Mary Helen Washington when she describes her plans - the work she intends to do in the next decade.

Three phases in black woman's History

Walker sees the history of the black women she would like to write about in three phases. The first would be the physically and psychologically abused black women who lived during slavery and Reconstruction. Such are the characters of Margaret and Mem Copeland in *The Third Life of Grange Copeland*. The second black women would be women of the nineteenth and twentieth century, like writers Phyillis Wheatley and Nella Larsen, who were groomed by black and white society to be "extraordinary," but who were torn by "contrary insights." Such is the character Meridian for she struggles through her familial history and the collective history of black people until by the end of the novel, *Meridian*, she begins to get well. The third black women Walker proclaimed would be the new black women who have held onto the creative spark within themselves and are able to recreate themselves in the context of their culture. Such a woman is Shug of *The Color Purple*, for she refuses to be thwarted by white racism or sexism within her black community. In a real sense Celie's growth and liberation combine all three phases of Walker's focus.

Not only are Walker's novels concerned with generations of black women who represent phases in the history of African-Americans, she deliberately uses characters from the past in her work. For example, in her innovative short story "Advancing Luna," Walker uses as a major character Ida B. Wells, the founder of the nineteenth-century Anti-Lynching Society who protested the lynching of black men for the alleged rape of white women. Through a dialogue with this nineteenth-century activist, the narrator of this story probes the complexity of sexism and racism in this country by telling the story of an interracial rape. In another story, "Source," Walker uses the slave narrative of a mixed-race woman, Luisa Pocquet, to shed light on the barriers that exist between contemporary dark-skinned and light-skinned black women. One of Walker's most interesting stories is "1955," which is about a blues singer, who, like Ma Rainey, had her song ripped off by a white singer. Its major character, Gracie Mae, clearly resembles Shug of *The Color Purple*. And one of Walker's best-known award-winning stories. "The Revenge of Hannah Kemhuff," is based on a true story about the Depression that Walker's mother told her.

Actually, many of Walker's stories, including the stories that are the basis for *The Color Purple*, came out of her family's history and the oral tradition. As is the case in many cultures, history of the folk is passed on through the telling of stories. Walker and other contemporary African-American women writers, like Toni Morrison and Gloria Naylor, have transformed these oral stories into a literary mode while preserving their historical content. In so doing, these writers embody history in stories even as they analyze its effects on the present and the future. The fiction of contemporary African-American women writers could be said to be the only recorded history of their mothers' and grandmothers' lives.

From Black Feminism to "Womanism"

In the early eighties, Walker began to use "womanism," a term she coined to name her philosophy of life. By then she was divorced from her husband, had lived in New York City, and had moved to San Francisco with her daughter Rebecca. She had begun her third novel, *The Color Purple*, had just finished two books, *You Can't Keep A Good Woman Down* (1981), her second collection of short stores, and *Good Night Willie Lee, I'll See You in the Morning* (1979), her third collection of poems, as well as an edited volume of Zora Neale Hurston's work. She had become a major articulator of black feminism through her teaching, speeches, political action, and literary work. Still, she felt the inherent tension in the term "black feminism" in that it represented sexism and racism as if they were two entirely separate phenomena, a fact that did not reflect her people's history or her experience.

For Walker, the term "feminism" evoked Western feminism with its history of privilege, while the term "black feminism" was imprecise and, to her, was awkward sounding enough to be the name of a "fly spray." She wanted a word that evoked the strength, passion, grace of black women's history of creativity and struggle. To her the word woman, a word traditionally used with respect among black folk, communicated these qualities more than femme, the root of the word, feminism.

"Womanism" defined

In the preface to her collection of essays, *In Search of Our Mothers' Gardens: Womanist Prose* (1985), Walker gives us a detailed definition of her new term. Clearly it evolved as she wrote *The Color Purple*, since she ends her description with the statement that "womanist is to feminist as purple is to lavender."

The term womanism epitomizes the process of Walker's growth from *Once*, her first book, to her most recent, *Horses Make the Landscape More Beautiful*, and indicates her pivotal position in the evolution of the Women's Movement of the eighties. In defining her new term, Walker combines critical elements of her work: the importance of black folk history and the centrality of female creativity and competence in that history as symbolized by the quilt; her belief in the oneness of life and the sacredness of nature so often embodied in her work by the image of the tree; the fusion of the sensual and the spiritual as inseparable from the demand for justice.

Walker tell us that womanist is derived from "womanish," a black folk expression used by mothers to female children "referring to outrageous, audacious, courageous or willful behavior." It is this view of woman, as a grownup, in contrast to the Western view that woman is a helpless incompetent, that Walker would like to pass on in her work.

Love of justice

Walker stresses that a womanist is not a separatist, that she makes connections where they exist-e.g., she sees the relationship between her preference for women's culture and the survival whole of an entire people, women, and men. She stresses that a womanist loves other women, sexually and/or non-sexually, but that sexual preference is not an essential part of her definition. Instead, what is essential is that she loves herself. It is that love of self that is the impetus for her commitment to women and men and to struggles for justice. Walker ends her definition with a chant in which the word love is predominant. A womanist, she chants:

Loves Music, Loves dance, Loves the Moon Loves the Spirit. Loves love and food and roundness. Loves struggle. Loves herself. Regardless

Walker's definition of a womanist highlights qualities that many people may not associate with feminism. At its core is a woman's love of herself that is integrated with her love for all living things. It is noteworthy that a womanist "Loves Struggle." It is this quality that is so evident in Walker's works - the capacity to ask those questions that are uncomfortable, even subversive, as a route to truth. Only when one trusts one's experience, tempered by the depth that history can give, can one truly love oneself. For Walker, this is an invaluable quality, so evident in African-American women's history. Without it, they could not have held onto their creative spark. Feminism as economic self-sufficiency or equality with men is incomplete without the qualities of honesty, willfulness, which are self-love.

Eroticism and spirituality

The other pivotal quality in Walker's definition is eroticism, a quality that at first glance seems at odds with feminism, which so often is defined puritanically. But for Walker and most contemporary African-American women writers, eroticism is one's right to fulfillment, of which sexuality is only one, however essential, ingredient. The right to sexual fulfillment for women has often been trivialized or denigrated in the West. But for African-American women writers like Walker, Toni Morrison, and Paule Marshall, eroticism is inseparable from spirituality. The body and spirit are one. For Walker, when we feel the quality of deep satisfaction in our lives, it becomes the will in us, as it does in Celie of *The Color Purple*, to change that which denies us freedom, so that we might continue to experience that fulfillment. personal fulfillment cannot be maintained if those around us lack it. So like Celie, once we achieve it for ourselves we will struggle to achieve it for those around us. Perhaps that is why *The Color Purple* is such a popular novel, for it is a graph of Celie's journey to that realization.

Yet Walker did not come to such a realization easily. There is a process of struggle in her work that refuses to ignore pain, violence, or oppression. As with Celie of *The Color Purple*, Walker's opus is a journey through that pain to the concept of womanism and the health that term underlines.

Experimentation with different genres

Walker has published in four different literary genres: the poem, the short story, the essay, and the novel. Drama is the only significant literary **genre** in which she has not published. The enumeration of her work in different **genres** is a key to her literary process, the way her work evolves. If one looks at her work as a whole, one can see how experimentation with different **genres** is a means by which she develops ideas.

In an interview, Walker observes that often an idea comes to her in a compressed form - the poem. If the idea keeps "bothering her," she may work with it in the form of short story or an essay. And if it refuses to go away it may become embodied in a novel. The novel is a form that demands much time and concentration. Walker seems to give way to it when an idea becomes so obsessive that she must work through its various contours.

Walker's works then should, ideally, be read as a whole. Many sections of her novels are related to poems. Examples include the section called "Indians & Ecstasy" in *Meridian*, which is related to a poem called "Eagle Rock" in *Revolutionary Petunias*. Many of the poems about *Nature in Good Night Willie Lee, I'll See You in the Morning* and *Horses Make the Landscape More Beautiful* are related to the **imagery** of *The Color Purple*. Often her short stories seem to be a transition between the poem form and the novel. So the short story "1955" in *You Can't Keep A Good Woman Down*, which is written in the diary form of a blues singer Gracie Mae, seems related to the character Shug, as well as to the letter form of *The Color Purple*. Sometimes Walker uses short stories to work through unresolved questions that have appeared in a novel, as in the short story "Advancing Luna," which refers back to the "Of Bitches and Wives" section in *Meridian*. Sometimes works about the same idea complement each other as in the case of the short story "Everyday Use," from *In Love & Trouble*, and the essay "In Search of Our Mothers' Gardens."

Walker's experimentation with different literary **genres** is similar to the use of different instruments in an orchestra that is doing variations on the same **theme**. Yet each of these genres, like different instruments, has its own unique sound that thereby changes the **theme**. In general, Walker's poetry appears to be the most personalized of her forms, while the short story form often uses ritual to explore a character distinct from herself. Her essays are more overtly analytical while her novels inevitably develop characters within the context of a community. In briefly analyzing those of her works written before and after *The Color Purple*, it is a good idea to keep in mind how she uses different **genres** to create various forms derived from a similar idea and how that idea grows, develops, is refined as she plays with it.

COLOR PURPLE

PLOT ANALYSIS

LETTER 1

The Color Purple begins with Pa's voice warning Celie not to tell anyone about his rape of her, especially her mother, signaling to us the way in which incest is shrouded in silence. By having Celie write to God, Walker initiates not only the **theme** of spirituality in the novel, but also Celie's feeling of isolation. Celie is just learning to write, hence she crosses out words and uses her own language rather than the standard English that she would have been taught. She writes in order to make some sense out of her experience. Like many incest victims, she does not know what is happening to her for she knows nothing of sexuality. Her mother, worn from childbearing, clearly does not grasp what is happening to Celie. By the end of the first letter, we know that the fourteen-year-old Celie is pregnant.

LETTERS 2, 3, 4

Celie confides to God that she had a baby, that her mother died, and that Pa has taken her baby away from her. She becomes pregnant again. Pa has gotten tired of her, begins looking at her sister Nettie, but finally marries another woman. In church, Mister is drawn to Nettie but Celie advises her to stick to her books.

LETTERS 5, 6, 7

These letters focus on Mister's courting of Nettie, Pa's refusal to give her to him, and Pa's offering of Celie instead. Walker emphasizes the way men are the primary actors in determining the future of their girl-children, and how in marriage women are a means of exchange between men. Mister enumerates Celie's qualities as if she were a slave he is selling, ending with a statement associated with slaves, that she tells lies. Mister desperately needs a wife, because his first wife has been killed by her boyfriend and he needs a woman to manage his home and his children.

An important note: In letter 6, Celie sees a picture of Shug for the first time and falls in love with this "Star's" beauty and independence, which is so different from her lot. She begins dreaming of Shug.

LETTER 8

As Nettie teaches her how to write, Celie recalls how in the past Miss Beasley, the schoolteacher, came to see her in an effort to persuade her father that she should come back to school. But Celie is pregnant, an absolute obstacle. This incident is important since it indicates that the black community, personified by a teacher, does inquire about Celie's welfare. But pregnancy halts all growth for a woman. Celie then comes back to halts all growth for a woman. Celie then comes back to the present, recounts how Mister, who barely looks at her, finally agrees to marry her because he is overcome by the mess in his home, and since Pa offers him a cow as well.

LETTER 9

Celie writes about her wedding day, about being injured by Mister's children who resent her as their new mother, and about going through the ordeal of sleeping with Mister it his loveless marriage. Only the thought of Nettie and Shug, her dream, get her through that experience.

LETTER 10

This is an important letter in that it is the first time Celie thinks she has news of her child, Olivia, whom she believes she sees with a black lady, the Reverend's wife. The letter also gives us a view of relations between blacks and whites, since the white storekeeper treats even this black lady as if she is a stupid girl. In this **episode**, we see Celie laugh, a side of her we haven't seen before.

LETTER 11

Nettie runs away from Pa and comes to live with Celie, but is constantly harassed by Mister. She spends the time teaching Celie how to write until the rejected Mister says she must go. She does, with Celie's advice that she go to the Reverend's wife and with her promise that "nothing but death" will keep her from writing Celie. This letter is the transition into the next phase in Celie's life as she is completely alone and yearns for Nettie's letters. The sisters see writing as the bridge between them, a key **theme** in the novel.

LETTER 12

In this letter (which begins "g-o-d," rather than "Dear God"), Celie recounts another visit to her from the outside world. Kate and Carrie, Mister's sisters, attempt to help Celie. They tell her about Ann Julia, Mister's first wife and about Shug Avery. They buy her the first new dress she's ever had and try to get the children to help her with the work. But Mister drives them away. Kate insists that Celie must fight but Celie asks "What good it do? I don't fight, I stay where I'm told. But I'm alive," as Celie reacts with the fear that has been inculcated in her.

LETTER 13

Harpo asks his father why he beats Celie. "Cause she my wife" forcefully and simply expresses the power relations between Celie and Mister; between husband and wife. Celie describes how she feels when Mister beats her: "I say to myself Celie, you a tree. That's how I know trees fear man," as Walker relates human beings' treatment of each other of Nature. Harpo tells Celie that he's in love with somebody he's never spoken to but whom he sees in church.

LETTERS 14, 15, 16

An excited Celie hears that Shug Avery is coming to town. She helps Mister get ready to meet her, in the first scene where they seem to have anything in common. Shug Avery is called "The Queen Honeybee", the kind of title blues singers are often given, a reference to the sweetness he name implies. Mister comes back from seeing Shug, has no news for Celie and leaves again. After he comes back, he sits on the porch, leaving Celie and Harpo to do the work, an indication that as master of his house he does not have to work unless he wants to.

LETTERS 17, 18

The father of Harpo's girlfriend says he's not good enough because her boyfriend killed his mother. Harpo has nightmares about his mother's murder, and he talks to Celie about his love for Sofia. Finally, he brings Sofia to meet his father. (Notice Celie's description of Sofia and how precise her language is.) Sofia is pregnant but is not worried about her well-being since she and her sisters are friends: Walker's comment on the solidarity of sisterhood. Sofia challenges Harpo as she observes the docile Celie. Harpo cannot talk with his father even though he is upset. Harpo finally marries Sofia and works harder than he ever has as he and Sofia build a home together. The final words of this letter indicate that Mister objects to the way Sofia seems to be on equal terms with Harpo.

LETTERS 19, 20, 21

In these letters, Celie recounts how, despite three years of marital happiness, Harpo wants to control Sofia. He is influenced by the social mores that call for a wife to be obedient to her husband. Mister advises Harpo that he should beat the uppity Sofia, and Celie agrees. But the strong Sofia fights back; she refuses to be hit. Celie has trouble sleeping because she knows she has wronged Sofia and is not at peace until she apologizes; Walker is showing us how women sometimes internalize their own oppression. In their conversation' Sofia describes to Celie how she came from a family of many brothers and had to learn to fight. She advises Celie to fight too. But Celie tells Sofia that she gets sick rather than mad, a reaction many people have when they repress their anger. Celie offers to make a quilt with Sofia, a sign of the peace between them. In these letters, Walker also gives us a picture of flexible gender definitions in relation to work. Often Sofia is doing carpentry and Harpo is taking care of the babies.

LETTERS 22-26

Mister brings Shug Avery home despite the town's bad talk about her. The scene of Celie and Shug's meeting is important. Celie is excited; Mister declares to Harpo that Shug should have been his mammy. And the sick Shug, anticipating trouble from Albert's wife, calls Celie ugly. We find in this section that Mister's name is Albert. Shug can call him by his first name, and indication of their equality. Celie nurses Shug to health and begins to admit to herself her physical attraction to this beautiful woman. Shug, at first, is difficult, but encouraged by Celie's kindness, and excellent cooking, she begins to get better. Walker makes this evident by having Shug begin to hum a song.

LETTER 27

Mister's father comes to see him, because he is upset that Shug Avery is living under Mister's roof. We see the power the father tries to exert over the son. His visit brings Celie and Mister close to each other as they both love Shug. Then Tobias, Mister's brother, comes to visit and tries to enlist Celie as an ally against Mister and Shug. But Celie, Mister, and Shug stand together. During his visit, Celie teaches Shug how to "stitch on a quilt." For the first time Celie "feel just right."

LETTERS 28-31

There is harmony among Sofia' Shug, and Celie that is symbolized by the quilt they're working on, called "Sister's Choice." But Harpo is upset because he can't control Sofia; he has been taught that this is the way a husband is supposed to act. He eats and eats to get bigger so that he can deal with his strong, muscular wife. Of course, this does not work. Sofia, disgusted with Harpo's behavior, leaves home, taking her children with her to her sister's. Her talk with Celie about how boring Harpo's lovemaking has become is the first conversation that emphasizes the right of woman to sexual fulfillment. Celie gives Sofia the quilt as she leaves with her sisters.

LETTERS 32, 33, 34

Celie tells us how Harpo changes after Sofia is gone. He makes plans to build a juke joint and finally persuades Shug to sing there. When Mister objects to his wife going to the juke joint, Shug makes it clear she is her own woman and insists that Celie come. Shug sings a song to Celie and Celie describes the desire both she and Mister have for Shug. Celie says Shug's song is "First time somebody made something and name it after me." Shug is now well and decides she must leave. But Celie is upset and tells her that Mister beats her, precisely because she isn't Shug. Shug says she won't leave until Albert stops beating her.

LETTER 35

This letter recounts Celie's initiation into sexual pleasure as Shug gives her a lesson on her body. Walker uses images from Nature to describe the beauty of the female body.

LETTERS 36, 37, 38

Celie recounts how Sofia got jailed. Sofia comes with her new husband to the juke joint. Squeak, Harpo's new girlfriend, hits Sofia and Sofia knocks her out. We see that Sofia refuses to be hit by anyone. This incident is a prelude to the letter in which Celie tells us how the mayor's wife says Sofia should be her maid. Sofia refuses and is hit by the mayor. Sofia responds by knocking the white man down. She is beaten and taken to jail. These letters also introduce Squeak to us. Celie insists that Squeak have Harpo call her by her right name-Mary Agnes. This is an important **theme** in the novel in that Celie understands how "Squeak" is diminished by not being called by her right name.

LETTERS, 39, 40, 41, 42

Sofia's family and friends meet to devise a plan to help her, after they learn she's to serve twelve years in prison. They discover that Squeak is related to the Sheriff as Walker points out the way many black and white folk in the South are family, in name only. They decide to have Squeak go to the Sheriff and tell him a false thing - that the worst punishment for Sofia would be to make her the mayor's wife's maid. At least, then, Sofia would not be in jail. Squeak is sexually assaulted by her own "uncle," but her visit does help to get Sofia's "sentence" changed. At the end of her ordeal, Squeak insists that Harpo call her by her real name, Mary Agnes. Six months later, Mary Agnes begins to sing.

These letters emphasize that black women, in this case Sofia and Squeak, are, like black men, physically assaulted when they resist racism. Interestingly, Walker demonstrates this in the context of two major stereotypes of black women - the "mammy" and the "slut." These letters graphically demonstrate how black families come together to help one of their own - and how they understand the way white folks think.

LETTERS, 43, 44, 45

These letters follow Sofia's life when three years later, she is let out of jail in the custody of Miss Millie, the mayor's wife. Sofia is enraged at white people and barely manages to be a maid. Her story indicates the distance between black and white women created by racism and the complex interactions of sexism and racism in Southern society.

The mayor buys his wife a car because "Colored" have cars. But he refuses to show her how to drive it. Miss Millie decides to have Sofia help her learn to drive and, in one instance, decides to drive Sofia home to visit her children, whom she hasn't seen in five years. Because Miss Millie cannot get her car to reverse, she becomes hysterical, refuses to let black men help her, and insists that Sofia come back home with her immediately. As a result, Sofia only gets to spend fifteen minutes with her children. Walker does these scenes in an ironic tone ending with Sofia's comment that "white folk is a miracle of affliction."

LETTERS 45, 46

Shug comes back for Christmas with a new husband, O'Grady. Both Mister and Celie are upset and jealous. Shug has become successful and has a big house in Memphis. She makes sure Mister doesn't beat Celie anymore and asks about her and Mister's love life, which hasn't improved.

LETTERS, 47, 48

Celie relates her life experiences to Shug-how she was raped by Pa, how nobody but Nettie had ever loved her, and that she hasn't heard from her sister for years. This scene ends with Celie and Shug making love. Walker uses images of mothering to describe their lovemaking; and not once does she use the word lesbian.

LETTER 49

This letter begins the next phase in Celie's life. Through Shug's intervention Celie gets one of Nettie's letters and learns she's been writing all these years.

LETTERS 50, 51

Shug flirts with Mister and finds out he's been keeping Nettie's letters from Celie. Celie is so angry she feels she could kill Mister with a razor while she is shaving him, but Shug prevents her. Shug tells Celie about her children, her romance with Albert, their children, his weakness in relation to his father, her conniving to break up his marriage with Annie Julia, her jealousy of Celie before she met her, in an attempt to figure out how Albert has become such a terrible person. Celie figures out that Nettie's letters are in Mister's trunk. She and Shug finally find them.

LETTERS, 52, 53, 54

Nettie's first two letters tell Celie about her flight from Mister, his attempt to rape her, and her finding Corinne, the Reverend's wife. Nettie thinks already that Albert will fulfill his promise of keeping her letters from Celie.

LETTER 55

Two months later, Nettie writes to say she's in Africa - that she's gone there with Corinne and Samuel as a missionary and that while she was in their town she saw the mayor's maid (who we know is Sofia), and that she acted very strangely. Nettie also tells Celie about the glorious history of Africa and about Olivia and Adam, supposedly Corinne and Samuel's children.

LETTERS, 56, 57

Nettie recounts her traveling on the train to New York City. She learns how many black people love Africa and give money to African Missionary Societies. She then describes Samuel, whom she clearly admires, and her trip to England. In her letter, Nettie recounts much African history, and asks how Africans could have sold other Africans, like her ancestors, to whites.

LETTER 58

Nettie tells Celie about her first sight of Africa. She lands in Monrovia and explains how African-Americans settled in the country of Liberia. Her excitement and joy about being in Africa are clear.

LETTERS, 59, 60

Celie and Shug now sleep together regularly. Celie is still enraged at Mister for keeping Nettie's letters from her. Shug suggests that she turn her attention from anger to making pants for herself.

LETTERS 61, 62, 63

Nettie describes her travel through the African landscape to the Olinka home where she, Corinne, and Samuel are going to live as missionaries. Nettie finds that the Olinkas are similar in some ways to black folk in the South-e.g., they love barbecue. She pays special attention to the women, and how the wives work for their husbands. She tells us how their history is linked to the worship of the roofleaf, from which they make everything they need.

LETTERS 63, 64, 65

Nettie gives Celie a detailed description of the daily life of the Olinkas and notes how they think girls should not be educated. We hear, in particular, about Tashi, one of Olinka girls who becomes a friend of Adam. Nettie also tells us about the beautiful quilt-like designs the Olinka men weave, an indication that gender-related work is culturally determined.

After Nettie has been in Africa for five years, a road is beginning to be built, as Walker indicates the initial phase of European colonialism, following the arrival of missionaries, on Olinka land. Nettie also mentions that Olivia and Adam look like her. She describes the Olinka funeral of Tashi's father, and tells Celie that although it is against their custom, Tashi's mother wants her daughter to be educated. Nettie points out that women are completely subordinate to their husbands, as Walker underlines that sexism in Africa preceded the arrival of Europeans. Walker makes it clear through Nettie's discussion that sexism in black society is not derived from racism.

LETTERS 65, 66, 67

Olinka land, now controlled by a British rubber manufacturer, is taken over by the road builders, the beginning of colonialism. Corinne has become very ill. There is tension between her and Samuel because Olivia and Adam look so much like Nettie that Corinne wonders whether Nettie had any relationship with Samuel before they took her into their home. Nettie realizes that Adam and Olivia are Celie's, when Samuel tells her about how he and Corinne got these children. Nettie discloses to Celie that their real father was lynched and that Pa was not their father.

LETTERS 68, 69

Celie is amazed by Nettie's news. She and Shug go to see Pa, who now has a new house and a new wife. Celie tells Pa what she has learned about her real father. Pa responds that it was too pitiful a story to tell little girls. He points out that he made sure he used a white man as a front for his business so that he might avoid the same fate as Celie's father, a ploy that some Southern black businessmen used to escape racist violence. Celie and Shug put markers in the area where her parents were buried, an act that consolidates their sense of themselves as each other's family.

LETTERS 70, 71, 72

Nettie describes Corinne's disbelief in Samuel's story about how he got the children, disbelief that is killing her. Using a quilt which has in it fabric Corinne bought the day she met Celie, Nettie reminds her of that meeting. Corinne finally remembers, but it is too late; she dies. (Note that Walker has Corinne mention that she is a graduate of Spelman.) Nettie tells Samuel about Celie.

LETTER 73

In this letter, Celie declares that she won't write anymore to God but to Nettie. Celie is disgusted with her idea of God. But Shug tells her God isn't a white man with long hair; God is everything and loves admiration. It is in this letter that Shug uses the image of the color purple to embody the unity and enjoyment that is her view of God, a view that sees no separation between the body and the spirit and expresses the spirit of the oneness of the universe. Celie's eyes are opened to this view, but she is still angry at what happened to her. She does as Shug suggests, and replaces her image of a white male God with a rock. "Every time, I conjure up a rock, I throw it."

LETTERS 74, 75

These letters are critical in the novel, for in them Celie tells us how she confronts Mister in the context of their family. Sofia has finally come home after eleven and one-half years and at her homecoming dinner both Celie and Squeak tell the men they are going North with Shug. Celie reveals to Mister that she knows about her children and warns Harpo that his treatment of Sofia was related to the trouble she has experienced with whites. Sofia says she will take care of Susie Q, Squeak and Harpo's daughter. When Mister tries to stop Celie from going North and verbally abuses her, she responds with a curse: "Until you do right by me, I say, everything you even dream about will fail." Celie's final words of this letter indicate how far she's come in believing in herself.

LETTER 76

The excited Celie tells Nettie about her life in Memphis. The details of her description are related to Walker's definition of womanism for they give us a view of a woman-centered household. Shug's light-filled house is round and surrounded by trees and flowers. Turtles and elephants, key animals in African mythology, are everywhere. In this harmonious universe Celie develops her own business of making pants. Walker demonstrates the creativity of supposedly ordinary black Southern women even as she underlines the joy in work that is creative rather than drudgery. Celie proudly ends her letter with the name and address of her business.

LETTER 77

This letter is interesting in that Celie comments on language (Walker's comment on her own process), and how one cannot express oneself in a language that is alien, even if that language is considered "correct." The image of Sofia jumping over the moon revises the old nursery rhyme.

LETTERS 78, 79, 80

Celie returns home in time for Sofia's mother's funeral and describes the changes there. Sofia's sisters as well as her brothers are pallbearers for their mother's funeral, indicating the strength and love of both sexes. Celie tells Sofia about how close Mary Agnes and O'Grady are and about "reefer," while Sofia regales Celie with stories about Mister, how he fell apart after she and Shug left, but that he and Harpo became friends, Walker's comment on the need for fathers and sons to relate through love rather than through the authority of patriarchy. Mister is now happier since he has sent Nettie's letters to Celie; he even works. Celie also mentions that Henrietta, one of Sofia and Harpo's children, has a blood disease, sickle-cell anemia.

LETTER 80

This is a long letter in which Nettie and Samuel leave Africa to get money for the Olinkas. She is now in England where she and Samuel have married. Nettie describes how the English have destroyed the Olinkas' main crop, the roofleaf, then forced them to pay for imported tin, a technique often employed by colonials. Some of the Olinkas resist by escaping to the forest. Nettie also describes their meeting a white woman, who is a wealthy, independent writer and who believes a war in Europe is coming. In England, Samuel talks a great deal about Corinne's background, her black and Indian ancestry, about the founding of Spelman and about famous black leaders. DuBoyce is probably W.E.B. DuBois.

Another plot begins to evolve in this letter. In England, Adam misses Tashi, though he is angry with her because she went through the female initiation of her tribe, which is a scarification ceremony.

LETTER 81

The story of Tashi and Adam continues. Nettie tells Celie that when they had returned to Africa, Tashi had hidden from them because she was ashamed of her scarification. Through Nettie's discussion of Tashi's situation, Walker protests the African custom of clitorectomy, female circumcision, far more complicated and dangerous than male circumcision. Clitorectomies are still common in certain parts of Africa today, where girls are not considered women until they have gone through this "ritual."

LETTERS 82

Celie tells Nettie that Pa has died and they have come into the property that was always theirs. Celie and Shug cleanse the house, chasing out the evil, and Celie tells Nettie she has a home to come to.

LETTERS, 83, 84

A sad Celie pours out her feelings to Nettie about how Shug loves somebody else and has left for six months. She adds that they are using Nettie's advice about using yams to treat Henrietta's sickle-cell anemia. Mister is clearly changing; he and Celie talk about their love for Shug and become friends. When he asks Celie to truly marry him, she tells him she's not physically attracted to men. To her they're like frogs, an image that recalls men's depiction in some fairy tales.

LETTER 85

Mister gives Celie a telegram, which states that Nettie and her family may have been drowned in a boat hit by the Germans. Celie is distraught.

LETTER 86

Nettie tells Celie that Tashi and her mother have joined the mbeles, the rebels in the forest. Later, Nettie finds out that Adam has gone after Tashi, She also talks about God, how he has become more of a spirit to her, and of how she and Samuel may found a church without idols. Nettie also worries about how her African-centered children will fare in a hostile America.

LETTER 87

This long letter concentrates mainly on Sofia's relationship with Eleanor Jane, the white woman she was forced to take care of when she was a child; on Shug's letter to Celie; and Celie's relationship with Mister. Eleanor Jane feels that Sofia is the only mother she's known and wants her to love her baby boy. Sofia feels nothing for Eleanor Jane's child and tells her so. This section is important because it goes against the old stereotype whites have of black mammies, that no matter how they're treated, they love all white children. Celie also pours out to her sister her love for Shug, who has written that she finally went to see her children, whom she had not been able to mother, and how one of them is working on an Indian reservation, another comment on the interrelationship of blacks and Indians, a **theme** that runs throughout the novel. Walker also implies that Celie's loving of Shug is one reason why she is able to go and see her own children. The rest of this letter is Celie's recounting of the developing friendship between her and Mister, based on their love for Shug and their attempt to know each other. A sign of Mister's growth is that he asks Celie to teach him how to sew. Walker revises the concept of gender-specific work, as a means of showing that friendship between people, whatever their gender, is based on mutual respect.

LETTER 88

Nettie writes to say Adam and Tashi have returned, Adam has married Tashi and has gone through the scarification ceremony in order to appease Tashi's fears.

LETTER 89

Celie hires Sofia to work in her store and Harpo does not object. Eleanor Jane helps Sofia in the store, despite the social custom that whites are not supposed to work for blacks. Shug writes to say she's coming home. Celie realizes she's learned during Shug's absence what she was supposed to learn: that love is not possession.

LETTER 90

This concluding letter begins with a new salutation to various aspects of the universe as God, indicating the harmony and peace Celie is experiencing. All of Celie's family including her children and her sister Nettie are united at a Fourth of July barbecue. The last sentences of this last letter show how happy and vital this family is.

MEANING OF WALKER'S SIGNING-OFF

Note that in ending her novel with thanks to the characters for "coming,". Walker signs her initials with the title "author and medium." This self-designation represents a tradition (since Homer) that an author is merely an intermediary through whom some larger force (inspiration? the divine Muses?) expresses the story. The word "medium" also connotes one who claims to speak with and for the spirits of the dead, as Walker surely does for her turn-of-the-century characters, including some of her own forebears, whose spirits have surely "come" to her.

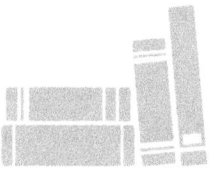

COLOR PURPLE

CHARACTER ANALYSIS

In discussing the characters of *The Color Purple*, it is important to keep in mind the form and structure of the novel. All the characters are presented to us through the letters that are the reflective voices of Celie and Nettie, the two sisters upon whom the novel focuses. All of the characters are related to these two sisters, either through strict or extended family ties. The way Walker develops her characterizations is a part of the novel's quilting process, for motifs, in the form of different characters, are reiterated so as to create a coherent pattern of repetition and variation.

CHARACTERS IN THE ORDER OF THEIR APPEARANCE

Celie

Celie is the focal character of *The Color Purple*. She is also its point-of-view character. Her letters compose the novel; even Nettie's letters are incorporated into Celie's letters. It is this Southern black girl's development from a frightened abused fourteen-year-old to self-assertive, middle-aged woman - that is the novel's subject. Her development and its causes are its focus. Celie's character then must be analyzed in terms of its different phases.

In the beginning of the novel, Celie presents herself as a compliant meek child who works hard, feels deeply, and has little regard for herself. Her profile is not too different from that of the ideal image of a girl during that period, except that she does not see herself as pretty, and she is decidedly black. She has learned to do many things competently in relation to housekeeping and caring for others; yet she cares little for herself. She is, in addition, the daughter of a distressed mother, who, we later learn, has been mentally affected after witnessing her first husband's lynching.

Nevertheless, even at the beginning of the novel, Celie has the potential for growth, as indicated by her subversive act of writing, through which she tries to make sense out of her life, a supposedly inconsequential life according to her society. Along with this reflective act, she has one other important attribute. She shares love with her younger sister, Nettie, whom she instinctively nurtures and protects. These two attributes, present even at the initial stage in the novel, are signs to the reader that she has the capacity to be more than she appears to be.

Although verbally silenced, Celie has the gift of storytelling. Like a few slaves, she has developed that gift through learning to write. Celie is also deeply spiritual, not in terms of established religion so much as in her identification with trees, with nature. Her characterization from the beginning of the novel is similar to that of her actual prototype, Rachel. She is "serviceable," that is, she exhibits her creativity in female folk forms-quilting, cooking, housekeeping-which are not only her means of survival but also of her spirit's nurturance.

Celie's desire for self-fulfillment is sparked when she sees a photograph of Shug, who has what Celie thinks she lacks- beauty, glamor, independence, self-confidence.

Celie, then, is a quiet, reflective girl, who tries to understand her life and desires more of it. She is nurturing and kind. She is observant and has a quirky sense of humor, as exemplified in her first meeting with Corinne. Above all, she is an instinctive storyteller - that is, she feels, without knowing why, that recording her observations is important.

What she lacks and develops through her relationship with Shug and Sofia is willfulness, the ability to fight, and insistence on her right to self-fulfillment. Celie is endowed with qualities we often associate with mothering-caring for others, selflessness. Walker implies through her characterization of Celie's development that if one is to be healthy these qualities must be balanced by self-assertiveness and the awareness of the self's right to pleasure.

When the novel ends, Celie is still a nurturing person, but this quality is balanced by her ability to be all she can be, particularly in her friendship with Mister. Above all, she is independent even from Shug, as she has transformed her skills and qualities, previously denigrated, into valuable sources of creativity; not the least of which is the writing and preservation of these letters.

Pa / Alfonso

Pa's voice is the first one we hear in the novel. He is presented to us, first, through the fourteen-year-old Celie's eyes and then, later, through her adult eyes. From the young Celie's perspective,

Pa is a powerful authority figure who rapes her, controls her and her sister's lives, and sells her off to Mister. Later, Celie learns that Pa is not her real father and that he has taken her real father's property. Then she depicts him as a shrewd businessman who accumulates wealth, builds a fine house, and marries two other women, both of whom are young girls.

He is a man intent on acquiring power sexually as well as in business. Pa is clearly an example of some black middle-class men at the turn of the century, who imitated white men and derived their definition of manhood from them. His striving for that status is symbolized by the mansion-like house he builds, based on his image of rich white men's houses.

Mama

At first, we hear little about Celie's mother except that she is ill and worn from childbearing. She dies when Celie is an adolescent. We learn later that Mama's mind was affected when she witnessed her first husband's lynching, and that she is isolated from her community because of her mental state. Pa marries her, takes her property, and makes a fortune from it.

Nettie

Nettie is Celie's younger sister. They share a love that inspires the letters which comprise the novel. Nettie is shielded by her older sister, is able to develop her intellectual capacity, and is perceived as prettier than Celie. She teaches Celie how to write, a hint of the teacher and missionary she would later become.

In the course of the novel, Nettie does not develop as much as Celie does. Rather, her letters are used to depict the relationships between African-Americans and Africans and to give much detailed information about African history. She functions most importantly as Celie's faithful sister and as the one who mothers Celie's children. As the educated one, she travels and has adventures, as many black women did, even at that time. Nettie also represents those women whose marriages are not only a meeting of bodies but also a meeting of minds.

The girl from round Gray

She is Pa's second wife and is important only because she prefigures Mister's marriage with Celie. Celie reports that "she walk round like she don't know what hit her."

Mister Albert

Mister is the most fully developed male character in the novel and in a sense is Celie's counterpart. Like her, he grows tremendously - from being an insecure and unhappy bully to a warm, thoughtful, and spiritual man.

In the beginning of the novel, Mister is presented, through Celie's eyes, as being similar to Pa, a symbol of authority and fear. But, as with Celie's characterization, we are given early clues to his potential for growth - primarily his love for Shug, for whom he must resist his father's wrath, something he has not been able to do for any prolonged period of time. His displaced anger vents itself on his wives and children. We are told, through Cassie and Kate, his sisters, about his unsuccessful marriage with Annie Julia, who was so neglected that she found a boyfriend over whom she was killed. When Mister marries Celie, it is primarily for the benefits of having an unpaid housekeeper and nursemaid rather than a lover and friend. Like many who are thwarted in love, Mister resents any strong love-bond between others-hence his withholding of Nettie's letters from Celie.

But he changes-first because his love for Shug is so intense that he takes her in when she is ill; then because he is left both by Shug and Celie when they discover he has withheld Nettie's letters. He is forced to confront himself, and the first result is his increasing closeness to his son Harpo.

Walker structures Mister's characterization so that he moves from being a patriarchal force to a person capable of being a father and of loving unpossessively. This change is signified in the novel not only by his growing friendship with Celie but also by his love of shells, and his learning to sew, a skill usually demeaned as woman's work. Just as Celie becomes a businesswoman, Mister learns to enjoy sewing, care for Henrietta, his grandchild, and appreciate nature.

The development of Mister's character is an indication that men are scarred by patriarchy, that change is possible, and that they too benefit from a world in which they do not nor are expected to dominate others.

Addie Beasley

She is the teacher who comes to persuade Pa that Celie should be allowed to come back to school. Like many teachers of that time she is unmarried; married women were forced by law to give up teaching. Pa makes fun of her because she is a spinster. When Miss Beasley sees that Celie is pregnant, she realizes there is nothing she can do; pregnant girls are not allowed in school. Both law and religion blame girls for such pregnancies, a sign of the double standards for women and men. Miss Beasley's visit is an indication that the black community inquires after Celie, a fact some readers miss. Interestingly, although Pa makes fun of Miss Beasley, he tells Mister that he plans to make a schoolteacher out of Nettie.

Corinne

She is the woman who, along with her husband Samuel, adopts Celie's children as well as Nettie and takes them with her to Africa. When we first meet her in the novel, she is presented by Celie as a lady, pleasant, dignified, and refined. Much of her characterization by Nettie consists of her profound jealousy that Nettie and Samuel have been involved-because Olivia and Adam resemble their aunt, a jealousy that eats away at her until she dies. She is convinced that these children are not Nettie and Samuel's only when Nettie shows her a quilt containing the fabric she bought the day she met Celie.

Corinne is characterized by Samuel as a Spelman graduate, an educated black lady concerned with the welfare of her race. Her aunt Theodesia, through whom Samuel met her, had also been a missionary. From a young age, Corinne was intrigued by her aunt's adventures. These polite and proper women "thought nothing of packing up for India, Africa, the Orient. Or for Philadelphia or New York." Corinne's characterization is Walker's way of emphasizing the "outrageous" things that black ladies have always done.

Corinne is also part Indian. Walker comments on the Cherokee Indians who hid out as "colored people" and eventually blended with them. Her quietness and rejection is attributed to her Indianness, a **theme** throughout the novel.

Carrie and Kate

These two women are Mister's sisters. They are important in the novel because they give Celie valuable information about Mister's first marriage with Annie Julia and about his continuing desire for Shug Avery. They also support Celie, by buying her first new dress and attempting to get the children to assist her in housework. Above all, they advise her to fight Mister to get the respect she deserves. Although they are Mister's kin, they nonetheless disagree with his treatment of his wife. Yet, because they are only his sisters, he can tell them to stop meddling in his home. Interestingly, Celie notes that Kate, who is older than she, and unmarried, looks younger: "Healthy, Eyes bright. Tongue Sharp."

Annie Julia

This first wife of Mister is presented to us first through the eyes of his sisters, then through Shug. Mister's sisters tell us that he left Annie Julia for periods of time while he was running after Shug. We learn from Shug that she intentionally interfered with Mister's marriage and that the neglected Annie Julia was killed by her boyfriend. Her characterization is important in that she is Celie's predecessor, her fate, a clear sign that it is Mister's love for Shug and his inability to oppose his father that account for his surly behavior.

Harpo

He is Annie Julia and Mister's oldest son, who initially resents Celie as his new mother so much that he hits her with a rock on her wedding day. He had been close to his mother, hence the nightmares he has about her, when he falls in love with Sofia. Like Celie, he is bullied by Mister who in turn has been bullied by his father. But Harpo desires a friendship/lover relationship with a woman, as is indicated by his love for Sofia.

For much of the novel, Harpo is married to Sofia. Walker characterizes him as a gentle man who loves his family and who regularly does the work needed to take care of his young children, even as his wife Sofia does carpentry. Through her portrayal of Harpo and Sofia's early marriage, Walker presents a good marriage based on respect rather than on fixed gender roles in relation to work. But the societal requirement that a husband should control his wife affects Harpo through the person of his father. Harpo's attempt to fulfill that requirement results in his unsuccessful attempts to beat Sofia and finally in the falling apart of his marriage.

Harpo is also a resourceful person. He builds the juke joint at which Shug sings. He aids Sofia when she is jailed, even though he is then involved with another woman. When Celie leaves, he becomes friends, for the first time, with his father and helps him to become emotionally healthy.

Harpo is representative of men who desire healthy, emotional relationships-with their fathers as well as with women. As a member of the third generation of males in his family, he represents Walker's affirmation that some men do not wish to dominate others, and actually have been affected by being dominated, but often are pressed by their fathers and peers to become patriarchal figures.

Sofia

When we first meet Sofia, she is described as a solid strong woman who accompanies Harpo to ask his father's permission so they might be married. Her reaction to Mister's demeaning remark about her pregnancy is a clear reflection of her character. She refuses to be frightened by him, and is self-assured because she has a strong bond with her sisters.

Sofia is physically strong, a quality that has often been denigrated in black women as being unfeminine, but a quality which Walker portrays as a positive attribute for women. The novel indicates that if women were as physically strong and as emotionally secure as Sofia, they could not be physically dominated by men; hence society's insistence that ideal women should be physically frail and emotionally dependent on men.

Sofia is representative of those women who refuse to be dominated by anyone: men, women, white society. She refuses to be hit and she chooses to do work at which she is competent, whether it is considered men or women's work. Often, such women have been negatively portrayed by society, a point of view that Walker overturns through her characterizations of Sofia. Sometimes, however, such women are severely punished for their "uppity" behavior. Sofia's marriage with Harpo is destroyed by his bending to society's dictum that he dominate her. She herself is almost destroyed by a racist system that brutally assaults her when she refuses to be Miss Millie's maid.

Walker's use of that tragic event is related to her debunking of the mammy stereotype so prevalent in white Southern society. Strong women such as Sofia were perceived primarily as workers, particularly suited to be white women's maids. In addition, Southern society projected the idea that there was nothing black women would rather do than to mother and love white children, a point that Sofia refutes in her relationship with Eleanor Jane. Sofia's story indicates the lengths to which white society would go to keep that belief intact. Sofia's experience clearly indicates that black women, as well as black men, who resist racism are physically attacked by white society.

Sofia is important in Celie's life not only as an example of a woman who refuses to be demeaned but also because she challenges Celie when she advises Harpo to beat Sofia. Through this confrontation, Celie learns how much she has internalized her fear so that it expresses itself in sickness rather than in healthy anger.

Shug/Lillie Avery

We first meet Shug through Celie's reaction to her photograph. That reaction tells us much about her character. Above all, she is a woman, in the full sense of that word, a point that Celie reiterates when Shug sings to her in the juke joint. We also see her through the eyes of Kate and Carrie when they tell us that she's "black as my shoe" and they are sick of her outlandish behavior. When we finally do meet her, Celie tells us that she's "dress to kill," and that her eyes look so feverish and mean, "if a snake cross her path, she kill it," an indication of her spiritedness as well as how much she has suffered. Her appearance in the novel is preceded by the preacher's sermon that she is an evil woman, Walker's comment on society's fear of Shug's eroticism.

Shug's name, which is short for Sugar, tells us how desirable she is; her pose in the photograph shows that she is sure of her worth, and her profession, that of a blues singer; that she is creative, and clear about her right to pleasure. She is Celie's guide to these possibilities. Because Shug is such a powerful figure, readers sometimes miss the point that she has struggled to become what she is.

We learn from Shug not only that she has been deeply wounded by Mister's inability to confront his father but that she schemed to destroy Albert and Annie Julia's marriage. She is prepared to dislike Celie because of jealousy. It is Celie's tenderness and nurturance that makes it possible for Shug to go beyond competing for Albert to developing a genuine bond with another woman. Celie's nurturance also makes it possible for Shug to seek out her and Albert's children whom she has not mothered, partly because she herself had not been protected and nurtured by her mother. In effect, Celie and Shug mother each other.

What Shug learns and gives to Celie is compressed into her statement that "God love admiration," and that "it pisses God off if you walk by the color purple in a field somewhere and don't notice it." Shug articulates the spiritual **theme** of the book - the oneness of nature, the inseparability of the erotic and the spiritual. This concept is central to the blues tradition, a distinctly black tradition, of which Shug is a representative. Sometimes that tradition is threatened by an anti-erotic strain of Christianity that attempts to teach women, Celie being one example, that to love God is to eschew the pleasure and innate goodness of life.

Walker's characterization of Shug as a woman in love with life enables the reader to experience the physical love between her and Celie as natural and fulfilling, a point of view contrary to society's definition of lesbian love as unnatural and limited.

One other important quality in Shug's characterization is the relationship between her creativity, her beauty, and her blackness. Mister and Celie are drawn to her as representing that deep part of themselves that they must fulfill if they are to become healthy. Throughout the novel, Shug insists on being all that she is. Like Walker's womanists she loves herself, regardless.

ODESSA

One of Sofia's strong sisters, it is Odessa who takes her in when she leaves Harpo, and helps to care for her children when she is in jail. Odessa is an example of the strong bonds of sisterhood, so focal in the novel.

Jack

Odessa's husband.

Mister's daddy

Like Pa, Mister's daddy is an example of men who define manhood in terms of domination and acquisition. It is he who dominates his son, Mister, and refuses to accept Shug. The one scene in which he is prominent gives us insight into his feelings about blackness. He negatively describes Shug as "black as tar," and "nappyheaded." As well, he tells us how central property is to him and how he uses his ownership of land as a threat: "This my house, This my land."

Tobias/Mister'S brother

Mister's brother is clearly under his father's control. Described as "a big yellow bear," he uses an apparently more friendly approach than his father to try to persuade Mister to get rid of Shug. He gives us a view of his society's definition of woman when he praises Celie for always working. If his wife were like that, he says, "Save me a bundle of money."

Swain

He is Harpo's friend who helps him to build the juke joint.

Henry Broadnax/Buster

He is Sofia's second husband, who is a prizefighter. It is important that Sofia insists that he not protect her in her fight with the police, for she knows that they could kill him.

Squeak/Mary Agnes

Squeak becomes the girlfriend of Harpo after Sofia leaves him. Her appearance is significant in that she is light-skinned, an attribute that Shug points out is admired by black men. She is kin to the warden and is raped by him in her attempt to help Sofia. She and Harpo have a child, Susie Q, and along with Odessa, she takes care of Harpo and Sofia's children when Sofia is in jail.

Squeak is important in the novel in that Celie and Shug help her to realize her potential. Celie tells her that Harpo should call her by her real name, Mary Agnes. Celie understands that the way people address each other is an indication of their power relations. Shug encourages Mary Agnes to sing in her own style, a means by which she can express herself and become economically independent. Later Mary Agnes becomes involved with O'Grady, Shug's husband, in whom she is no longer interested. As the "mother" of Sofia's children, and as a major element in helping to reduce Sofia's sentence, Squeak becomes one of the family.

The Mayor

He is one of the few white characters in the novel, and as mayor he is a representative of the official system of the South. He slaps Sofia when she refuses his wife's offer to hire her as her maid. As a white man, he assumes the right to hit a black person, even a woman. When Sofia knocks him down, she is assaulted by the police and taken to jail. But the mayor not only feels he has total control over blacks, he also has little regard for his wife's intelligence. Although he slaps Sofia when he thinks she has insulted his wife, he buys Miss Millie a car only because "even colored have cars," and then refuses to teach her how to drive.

Miss Millie / The Mayor's Wife

This white woman assumes that any colored woman would be glad to be her maid, an arrogance that precipitates Sofia's tragedy. Later Sofia describes her as incompetent. What happens when she has Sofia help her learn to drive, and yet is afraid to have black men help her when she can't reverse, is an example of the racism and cruelty practiced by Southern white women. Sofia only gets to spend fifteen minutes with her children for which Miss Millie thinks she should be grateful. Clearly, the bond of motherhood does not transcend racism. She is portrayed as a spoiled hysterical child.

The Warden

Although he is her uncle, he rapes Squeak when she goes to see him about Sofia's sentence, an indication of how the erroneous stereotype of the black woman as slut evolved.

Eleanor Jane/Mayor'S Daughter

We first meet her as a young child, then as a young woman who feels Sofia is the only mother she's ever had. She is upset that Sofia does not love her son Reynolds. Eleanor Jane is an example of whites who say they love blacks, yet she has never asked why Sofia was a maid in her mother's house. When she does find out, she stays close to Sofia by working with her in Celie's store. Sofia implies that this situation won't last since it violates the mores of the white community for whites to work for blacks.

O'Grady

He becomes Shug's husband, then later Mary Agnes' lover. He is portrayed as a reefer-smoking man.

Olivia

Olivia is Celie's daughter whom Corinne adopts and takes to Africa and whom Nettie helps to mother. She seems wise beyond her years.

Adam / Omatangu

Adam, Celie's son, falls in love with Tashi, an Olinka girl. Their love story is couched in the context of scarification ritual and clitorodectomies. He takes on an African name when he marries Tashi and is clearly as thoughtful and gentle as Samuel, the man who fathered him.

Samuel

Samuel is Corinne's husband for much of the novel. He is described by Nettie as a gentle, thoughtful and dignified man who regards his wife as a friend as well as a lover. He and Corinne knew each other from childhood as both were the relatives of women missionaries. From a young age he has a deep sense of values. He is a minister, concerned with the welfare of black people, and is kind and considerate to all. He marries Nettie after Corinne dies.

Catherine

She is the mother of Tashi, who asks, after her husband dies, that her daughter be educated. The request was not in keeping with

Olinka tradition but an indication that some African women saw the value of education for their daughters.

Tashi

Tashi is at first Olivia's best friend in Africa. Later she and Adam fall in love. She runs away to the forest after her scarification ritual because she is afraid Adam will be ashamed of her. He goes through a similar ceremony to assure her that he loves her. She is presented as an honest, forthright, intelligent young woman.

Daisy

She is Pa's second wife who tells Celie that the house rightfully belongs to her and Nettie. Interestingly, one of Zora Neale Hurston's minor characters in Their Eyes Are Watching God is a dark-skinned, much-admired young woman called Daisy.

Jarlene and Darlene

These twins help Celie with her business in Memphis. They also try to get her to change the way she speaks, which Celie resists.

Doris Baines

She is the white woman writer who has lived long in Africa and tells Nettie and Samuel about the upcoming war. She is clearly an early feminist.

Henrietta

She is the daughter of Harpo and Sofia who has sickle-cell anemia, a disease that some African-Americans have because their ancestors developed in Africa a biological means of countering malaria. Nettie tells Celie to treat it by feeding her lots of yams.

Germaine

He is Shug's young lover for a while. Through their relationship, Celie learns to be content without Shug.

James

He is Shug's son who lives in Arizona among the Indians and is called the black white man. He is the only one of her children who would see her.

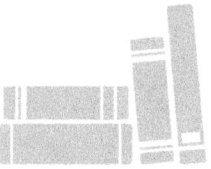

COLOR PURPLE

CRITICAL COMMENTARY

SOURCES AND THEMES

What Alice Walker has told us about her sources for *The Color Purple* is useful in understanding the novel. Her plans for her work in the 1970s, as discussed with critic Mary Helen Washington, suggested that her third novel would begin where *Meridian* had ended, that it would be contemporary in setting. Yet, *The Color Purple* is set in the early part of the twentieth century and could be called a historical novel. Walker has said that her third novel represented a detour; still it is a contemporary novel in that it addresses contemporary issues with which African-American women's literature and the international women's movement have been intensely concerned: issues of men's violence against women, issues of sisterhood, women's eroticism and lesbianism, and issues of women's economic independence. These issues have been discussed more openly during the eighties than ever before and Walker's *Color Purple* has been a significant contribution to that discussion.

Walker tells us in an interview that one source of the novel is a story her sister had told her, about two black women in rural

Georgia who were involved with the same man and who became so close they wore each other's panties. She also has said that Celie and Mister are based on her grandmother and grandfather, whom she had written about in the poem "Burial." Rachel had died young, her spirit so battered, no one ever really knew her. Walker wanted to give new life to this maternal ancestor of hers, a way of celebrating the many ancestors who had suffered greatly yet had survived and flourished.

CHARACTERS DIRECT THE AUTHOR

Walker has also told us in her essay "The Writing of The Color Purple" that she began the novel while she was living in New York City. But the characters simply refused to speak. They felt uncomfortable with the city environment, the noise, the buildings, the way city folks talk. They did begin speaking a little when she moved to San Francisco but even there they were reluctant to show themselves, because of constant interruptions in her life. Only when Walker devoted her undivided attention to them and moved to a place in the country, where the California landscape resembled rural Georgia, did her characters speak to her for long periods of time. And even there they insisted that she slow down her pace, take long walks, and mingle with Nature.

Walker's description of the emergence of her characters' voices indicates how important the oneness of creation, as symbolized by the color purple, is to the novel's **theme** and to its title. For as she immersed herself in the countryside she realized that although one does not usually think of purple as a prominent color in Nature, it is everywhere if one only takes the time to see it. As well, the language that her characters speak is related to the natural setting in which they live.

WALKER AS AFRICAN GRIOT

The Color Purple is characterized by its quiet tone, not only because its setting is rural Georgia but also because its characters, Walker says, came to her in dreams. She acknowledges that source in her dedication of the book to the Spirit, without whom these characters would not have revealed themselves to her. Theirs are the voices of ancestors who had been excluded from official history and who insisted on being heard. Like the African belief that the dead live as long as they are remembered, this novel gives Celie and Mister, Harpo and Sofia a way to live through the memory of their descendant, Alice Walker. As writer, Walker is a literary descendant of the African griot who recited the oral history of the ancestors to those who lived in the present. In imagining *The Color Purple*, Walker uses literature to give form to the history of her family.

The Color Purple is also an integral part of contemporary African-American women's literature. During the 1970s, essays like Audre Lorde's "The Uses of the Erotic" emphasized the importance of woman's sexuality to her liberation. In many ways, the character Shug is Walker's response to Toni Morrison's riveting character Sula, who in the novel Sula questions society's concept of good and evil in relation to woman. As well, Sula is one of the most compelling portrayals of female friendships, a major **theme** in *The Color Purple*.

Walker's third novel also responds to previous African-American women's literature, especially to Zora Neale Hurston's *Their Eyes Were Watching God*. That novel is one of the finest explorations of the relationship between woman's eroticism and self-fulfillment as well as a marvelous literary appearance of Black English, a variety of which Walker uses so adroitly in her novel. *The Color Purple* goes even further back in its formal origins. It reiterates the basic form of the slave's narrative, a major **genre** in nineteenth-century African-American literature, for the novel is a first-person narrative of Celie's journey from enslavement to freedom that uses phases of growth, predominant in the slave's narrative **genre**, not the least of which is the use of writing as a means to freedom. Walker reenvisions this form by demonstrating how this black woman's journey to freedom is not only from the enslavement of racism but also of patriarchy.

INCEST AND VIOLENCE

The Color Purple is not the first African-American novel to present scenes of incest or to focus on black men's violence towards black women. Ralph Ellison's *Invisible Man* and Toni Morrison's *The Bluest Eye* included scenes of incest. Richard Wright's *Native Son*, and Ann Petry's *The Street*, to name a few, depicted violence between black men and women. What differentiates *The Color Purple's* treatment of these two subjects from previous novels is Walker's use of Celie's voice. That is, these experiences are told from the point of view of the victim who at first does not know what is happening to her. Also, Walker does not attribute male violence-as other novelists have or as she did in *The Third Life of Grange Copeland*-to poverty or solely to racism. She emphasizes the physical power which men, whatever their class or race, have used over women.

WOMAN AS MULE

If we look at Walker's entire body of writing, we can also see how *The Color Purple* proceeds from her previous work. At the beginning of the novel, Celie resembles the Copeland women of Walker's first novel in that her body and spirit are battered, and she is seeking a language through which to articulate her condition. "Burial," and other poems in *Revolutionary Petunias*, are compressed narratives of rural Southern women and men that are developed in *The Color Purple*. Walker experiments with the letter/diary form as early as "Really, Doesn't Crime Pay" in *In Love & Trouble* and as recently as "1955" in *You Can't Keep a Good Woman Down*. Like Roselily in *In Love & Trouble*, Celie wonders "if she will ever know what it is to live," and like Hannah, in "The Revenge of Hannah Kemhuff," Sofia is almost crushed by racism. Poems in *Good Night Willie Lee* relate directly to the image of woman as mule, a central motif in this first half of *The Color Purple*. And like Meridian, Celie is haunted by the loss of her children.

Perhaps the most significant precedents in Walker's previous work are her experimentation with the form of quilting, and the "bodacious" spirit of the two publications that precede *The Color Purple*, a spirit arrived at only through the struggle so beautifully expressed in her early work. This spirit is embodied in the blues singer, Gracie Mae Stills, of "1955," the singer who is a **foreshadowing** of Shug. *The Color Purple* is one of a few novels in the tradition of African-American literature which explores the female blues singer as heroine. Like Walker's other novels, it is intensely rooted in the history and creativity of black women even as it pushes that tradition to another level. And as in her other two novels, Walker uses that history to explore change in generations of one black Southern family. In contrast to the sharecropping Copeland family of her first novel, or the small town Hill family of her second novel, Celie's family is a middle-class land-owning black family, like many at the turn of the century. Walker explores in her novels the relationship of class to racism and patriarchy. *The Color Purple*, then, does not come out of nowhere. It is informed by Walker's own work, as well as by the tradition of African-American Literature.

FORM: THE LETTER AS A FEMALE GENRE

One of the most arresting aspects of this novel is its form, a tour de force in that it is written entirely in letters. Letters are short units, each of which is complete in itself and, when stitched together with other letters, creates a series of patterns-a quilt. Just as important, letters tell us about the objective conditions of a person's life while being a subjective reflection on her life. The letter is a form of narrative that combines both the objective and the subjective. This dual quality may be one of the reasons why letters were written so consistently by women of the past, when their experience was considered trivial and was usually omitted from history. Through writing letters, women not only recorded their lives but also reflected upon them, a source of personal growth. Feminist historians have used women's letters as an important source of researching women's history in its concreteness as well as in its subjective ramifications. Walker has adopted this **genre**, so useful in history as a specifically female literary genre.

FORM: THE SLAVE NARRATIVE

But letters can be arranged in many different ways as the European tradition of the epistolary novel indicates. Walker arranges the letters of *The Color Purple* in terms of the African-American literary tradition, specifically the **genre** of the slave's narrative, which usually traced the slave's growing awareness of her oppression, her increasing resistance, escape, and the final realization of freedom in body and spirit. Like the slave in the nineteenth-century narratives, Celie's body and spirit are brutalized, a fate she accepts until she is confronted with other models, in this case Sofia's resistance through fighting, Shug's resistance through loving. Then there is a period of anger, followed by one of flight, her subsequent escape to Memphis where she develops here economic independence. Finally, there is a resolution of the spirit as she achieves independence of self, even from Shug, and effects the unification of her family and community. By ending her novel with a family reunion on the Fourth of July, Walker recalls Frederick Douglass, one of the finest writers of the slave's narrative, and the creator of the famous Fourth of July Speech that protested the institution of slavery.

BLACK GEORGIAN ENGLISH

The other unmistakably formal quality of this novel is Walker's use of Black folk English, a variety that is Black Georgian. It is extremely important to note that the Black English in this novel is not an all-encompassing Black English, but a variety that differs from say, the rural Floridian Black English of Hurston's *Their Eyes Were Watching God* or the urban New York English of Toni Cade Bambara's stories or June Jordan's novels. Celie's language is the essence of Black Georgian English as Walker transforms speech into a compressed written form.

Black English exists wherever Black people speak English- in various parts of the United States, the Caribbean, or Africa. It is a re-creation of British English critically affected by African **syntax** and sound, and by the use of **metaphor**. In addition, the environment of the particular group of blacks affects the English they speak, so that Jamaican English is both similar to and different from Georgian Black English. Specific historical experience has a strong bearing on the way language develops. There are some general qualities of Black English that are worth noting. As poet June Jordan notes in one of her essays, the passive voice is seldom used in Black English since someone is always seen as being responsible for a particular action. Verbs are used not only in terms of time but in relation to mood and the inflections of the voice that are indicated by various versions of "to be," as in "be's." Paramount to this language is the use of Nature, in its many aspects, as metaphor.

By having Celie speak in her own language, rather than in standard English, Walker demonstrates how a person's language is critical to who they are, how they think, and how they articulate their condition. By giving Black English a written referent, Walker helps to validate this language-rather than leaving it with the status of incorrect or bad English, a label with which it has often been denigrated.

BLACK ENGLISH CONTRASTED WITH STANDARD ENGLISH

Walker demonstrates the richness of this language by contrasting it with the staid standard English of Nettie's sections so that we can see how blacks have transformed a language not originally theirs into a unique version of English. Imagine Celie's first letter in standard English! In her own language, one can feel the depth of her confusion, the spareness of her environment. As writer, Walker transforms the oral language of Black Georgians into its essence, preserving for us, as Zora Neale Hurston preserved Black Floridian English, the values of Black Georgian society. And Walker resists the hegemonic power symbolized by standard English, by presenting, in intense compressed form, the images and sound of African-Americans, politically oppressed in the United States, but creative and rich in cultural forms.

One other significant aspect of the letters in *The Color Purple* is that they are not dated. Since using dates is such a common

convention when writing letters, that omission must have been intentional. By not dating Celie's letters, Walker gives them wider applicability in that they are not fixed in early twentieth-century Southern America. Celie's situation applies to many women in the present, and beyond the North American continent. *The Color Purple*, then, is not a historical novel in the usual sense, in that it is not limited by facts, dates, and geography.

IMPORTANT HISTORICAL BACKGROUND

Class and race issues

Many people miss the fact that *The Color Purple* is not about a poverty-stricken black Southern family. Pa and Mister both are landowning blacks, of which there were many in Georgia at the turn of the century. In focusing on this class, Walker reminds us that many Southern blacks were economically successful during Reconstruction, though because of the Southern racist system, some were eventually dispossessed of their property.

In the case of *The Color Purple*, Walker does a critique of patrimony and how it is linked to the pursuit of power. Mister owns land that he has received from his father who, in turn, received land from his father, who was a white slaveowner. Mister's father objected to his relationship with Shug Avery, a woman who refuses to be owned. Mister doesn't marry Shug and complies with his father's wishes partly because his father determines whether or not he will inherit land. In a real sense, Celie's abuse is derived from that fact, for Mister gives up the woman he loves, and becomes a bully to his first wife as well as to Celie.

Walker demonstrates how the pursuit of power that patriarchy represents affects the sons as well as women and how profit supersedes human needs. And she refuses to ascribe the sexism of black men solely to the effects of poverty, a position that has often been taken by black ideologues. Instead, she graphically traces how power determines the relationships among black men, between black men and women, as well as between the black community and white society.

Meanings of "Mister"

"Mister" is a title by which all white men at that time demanded that they be called by blacks. In turn, whites never gave blacks the title of "Mister," no matter what their class or age, and instead called them by their first names. This practice was a way of denigrating blacks, and labeling them as children, as inferiors who could never be equal to adults. In turn, many black men, regardless of class, insisted that their wives call them "Mister." They restored their wounded pride by imitating the practice of white men on whom they based their definition of manhood. In an interview, Walker reports that her grandfather insisted that his wife always call him "Mister." This is why Walker calls her character in *The Color Purple* "Mister;" many black men, like him, treated their families the way white men treated them. Through the character of "Mister," Walker shows us the intersections of racism and sexism in black society.

POWER: CLASS, RACE, GENDER

One other important aspect in the novel of this class/race/gender intersection has to do with how women, no matter what their class, are subordinated to men. Celie's real father was a businessman, who, because of his success, was lynched by white men, not an uncommon occurrence at that time. Her mother inherited the property but could not, because she was a woman, avail herself of it. Thus, the property passed to Pa, her second husband, who kept it when she died. In effect, that property actually belongs to Celie and Nettie, their parents' heirs. But because of their mother's second marriage, and the silence about their real father, who died violently, they are completely under the control of Pa. In addition to their economic dependence, this situation results in incest. As Walker has pointed out, then and now, "incest" often occurs between a mother's boyfriend, new husband, etc., and young adolescent children. The pursuits of power in the spheres of class, racism, and sexism are interrelated in the novel.

WOMAN'S STATUS AT TURN OF CENTURY

In order to understand how typical and/or atypical Celie's experience is, we need to consider a few facts about woman's status at the turn of the century. In much of the world, as well as in the United States, woman was seen as inferior to man. She did not have many of the rights we now take for granted. As recently as the nineteenth century, many American women could not be legal agents and thus could not own property or negotiate contracts, except through their fathers, husbands, or brothers. American women could not act as political agents; they could not vote or be elected to political office. They were not expected to speak in public or operate in the public domain and were to remain primarily within the family. They were not regarded as economically independent. "Respectable" women were not expected to work, particularly if they were married and had children. And women's goal in life was supposed to be marriage and motherhood.

In effect, women, "the weaker sex," were under the control or "protection" of their male relatives, and in many ways were conceived of as property. Husbands and fathers could not be prosecuted for physical or sexual abuse, and in many states, fathers, rather than mothers, had the right to children. Incest then, as now, existed although it was not often spoken about-young orphaned girls were considered particularly unfortunate since they had no access to power or even to protection. The Women's Rights movement of the nineteenth century protested these conditions but it took some fifty years to achieve the vote for women.

One aspect of woman's condition critical to Celie's story was the denial of education. Ironically, it was the creation of The Freedman's Bureau, which taught one and one-half million blacks to read and write between 1864 and 1870, that resulted in general public school education for poor Southern whites and women. But because of the passage of segregationist laws, blacks did not have equal access to education. Being able to read and write was considered as valuable a prize as it had been for slaves.

USE OF "MULE" IMAGE

Black women, of course, had an even lower status than white women, who were often placed on a pedestal, even as they lacked independence. *In Their Eyes Were Watching God*, Hurston characterizes the status of black women as that of a mule, an animal bred to work; creating an image that comes out of slavery. Walker makes great use of this image in the first part of *The Color Purple* as well as in the section set in Africa.

This is not to say that black women did not oppose these conditions in many different ways. Walker presents three different ways in which black women resisted their lot. Sofia represents the strong black woman who does not accept the definition of woman as weak and helpless and resists whites' attempts to diminish her. Often women like her have been denigrated both in black and white society as Amazons, or matriarchs, and punished for their resistance. Nettie represents women who did not marry but became missionaries, leaders, etc., and who used education as a means to transcend the low status of the black woman. As well, Walker uses Nettie to demonstrate the long history of relationships between African-Americans and Africa. Often these women had to separate themselves from their families and become "exceptional" women. Shug represents another avenue, that of the blues tradition, an area in which black women could express their creativity and eroticism, and be economically independent. Though maligned as immoral by the middle class, female blues singers were often seen by other blacks as queens. They were openly sexual, often bisexual, and explored pleasure as a woman's right. They, too, risked the possibility of separation from their children and experienced volatile economic changes in the music business as well as intense racism from the white world. That few novels, until recently, have used female blues singers as central figures indicates the ambivalence with which particularly the black middle class has related to these women. Their economic independence, overt eroticism, and spiritedness subverted the society's definition of the good woman.

STRUCTURE

In analyzing the plot sequence of *The Color Purple*, a discussion of its structure is extremely useful. The novel is divided into three parts: Celie's letters to God, Nettie's letters to Celie, and the interplay between Celie and Nettie's letters to each other. The structure is integral with the novel's **theme** of sisterhood. Celie wrote to God because she was alone, since Mister withheld Nettie's letters from her. Celie comes to know about Nettie's letters because of Shug's intervention. And finally Celie is able to respond to her sister who then replaces God as her audience.

Walker also traces Celie's growth through her relationship with three women and three men. Sofia, Shug, and Nettie represent different kinds of sisterhood. Nettie is Celie's blood sister, with whom she shares childhood, and who gives her the gift of writing. Sofia is the sister who shows her how to fight, and Shug is her lover/ friend who gives her love and pleasure and insists on her right to self-fulfillment. There are also three important men in Celie's story: Pa, her stepfather, who rapes her, disinherits her, and gives away her children; Mister, her husband, who beats and bullies her but who eventually grows into a person capable of love; and Harpo, who tries but cannot be like his father, and who begins to understand the importance of an equal relationship with women.

In analyzing the novel's plot, we will use this structure as well as numbers for the letters since there are no chapter headings. And in keeping with the tone of the novel, the language used for this plot will be as succinct as possible.

CRITICS RESPOND TO THE NOVEL THE COLOR PURPLE

The critical response to the novel *The Color Purple* has gone through many phases; reviews that were written immediately after its publication (1982-83); reviews that followed its being awarded the Pulitzer (1983 on); and assessments done in comparison to the film (1986 on). Also, there has been a steady stream of scholarly analyses of the novel, indicating its importance in American Literature. Not since the publication of Richard Wright's *Native Son*, in 1941, have there been such vociferous and varied responses to an African-American novel from black as well as white American society.

The Color Purple was published in June 1982. Its release was heralded by Gloria Steinem's interview with Alice Walker in the June issue of *MS*. Steinem is a founding member of *MS*. and a leading white woman activist. Her interview with Walker was placed next to a succinct piece by the black literary critic, Mary Helen Washington. The latter article concerned Walker's mother and her significance in the writer's work. A large picture of Walker's face, underlined by the caption, "Alice Walker, A Major American Writer," was featured on *MS.*'s cover, a portent of the media attention she would receive once the novel was released.

HURTFUL REVIEWS BY BLACK MEN

In her assessment of Walker's earlier works, Gloria Steinem pointed out that "a disproportionate number of people who seek out Walker's sparsely distributed books are black women," and that a "disproportionate number of her hurtful, negative reviews have been by black men." After the publication of *The Color Purple*, Walker's many books would be widely distributed; however, her most negative reviews would continue to be those by black men. Steinem emphasized in her review of the novel its kinship with Russian novels, its irresistible style of storytelling, its remarkable use of black folk English and the intersections of sex, class, and race that the novel explores.

In the following months, the novel received high praise, particularly for its poetic language and its innovative form, from reviewers in national commercial magazines such as *Newsweek* and intellectual and political journals such as *The New Yorker* and *The Nation*. Mel Watkins, a black reviewer for *The New York Times*, called Walker "a lavishly gifted writer." He was taken with "the density of subtle interactions among the characters," and "the authenticity of [the novel's] folk voice." He noted, however, "weaknesses in the novel," what he called "the pallid portraits of the males," and that Nettie's letters seemed like "mere monologues of African history." These are points that would be made about the novel in other reviews. Watkins ended his review with a superlative comment: "These are only quibbles however about a and striking consummately well-written novel."

CALLED "A CLASSIC"

During the rest of 1982, *The Color Purple* received similar praise in mainstream publications. But black feminist critic Barbara

Smith, in her review for *Callaloo*, a respected black literary journal, wondered if many of the reviewers had actually read the work. Her review, called "Sexual Oppression Unmasked," was submitted in October 1982 but was delayed for publication until fall 1984. In it, Smith focused on the womanist aspects of the novel. She called *The Color Purple* a classic because it does something new: "what Walker has done for the first time is to create an extended literary work whose subject is the sexual politics of black life, as experienced by ordinary blacks." Smith also pointed out that "no black novelist until Alice Walker in *The Color Purple* has positively and fully depicted a lesbian relationship between two women, set in the familiar context of a traditional black community." Smith ended her review with a provocative comment: "[*The Color Purple*] offers an inherent challenge to the Black community to consider fighting for the freedom of not just half but the entire race."

"A WOMAN'S WOMANIST BOOK"

Praise for *The Color Purple* as a womanist novel characterized reviews by other black women-Dorothy Randall-Tsuroto's review for *The Black Scholar* (published in Summer 1983, but apparently written before the novel received the Pulitzer), and Yvonne Porter's review for *Colorlines*, written just as Walker was awarded the Pulitzer. Porter began her review with the statement that "*The Color Purple* is a woman's womanist book..." She did warn her readers that some of them may be disturbed by Celie and Shug's sexual relationship, and reminded them that "lesbianism is an aspect of the black woman that has seldom been dealt with in any depth."

"BOURGEOIS"

These positive reviews by black women were followed by others during 1982-84, not all of which were entirely complimentary. Maryemma Graham in the Summer 1983 issues of Freedomways called *The Color Purple* Walker's "most compelling and thought-provoking work to date." But Ms. Graham thought that Walker identifies men as the sole source of female oppression, a view with which she disagrees. Graham also objected to the lesbian **theme** in the novel which she thought might "muddy the waters" about female bonding. Her major objection to the novel was that it is bourgeois, that "Walker has imbued her rural Georgia females with the strivings and potential for self-indulgence of the urban middle class."

WHITE STEREOTYPES?

Another review by black woman critic Trudier Harris, in Black American Literature Forum, asked whether Walker hadn't reiterated white stereotypes of both black women and men. Ms. Harris, who had previously written essays on Walker's earlier work, was clearly disturbed by the characters of *The Color Purple*.

During 1982-84, black male writers also discussed Walker's works. David Bradley wrote a long piece (which included an interview with Walker) on all of her work, for *The New York Times Magazine*, January 1984, called "Telling the Black Woman's Story." It was probably the first time a lead piece in that magazine featured a black woman writer. Bradley's overview of Walker's work was more his reaction to her personality than an analysis of her writings, a point that readers addressed in subsequent letters to the Magazine. Bradley clearly had not studied Walker's work and readers wondered why he had been chosen to do such a piece. What came through in his piece was how intrigued by and ambivalent he was about Walker's vision.

By 1984, Walker's literary achievements were being related to the black female literary tradition of which she is a part. In November 1984, *Ebony*, the black middle-class popular magazine, not usually a journal which features literary discussion, ran a piece "Black Women Novelists: New Generation Raises Provocative Issues." Beside a photograph of Alice Walker were those of other contemporary black women writers, Ntozake Shange, Toni Morrison, Paule Marshall, Toni Cade Bambara, and Gloria Naylor, who had recently won an American Book Award for her first novel, *The Women of Brewster Place*. *Ebony* also featured photographs of older writers, Margaret Walker and Ann Petry. The idea of a specific tradition of African-American women writers was a relatively new one in literary and academic circles. Walker's *The Color Purple* accelerated the pace with which that idea was promoted in nonliterary publications.

Scholarly journals, as well, devoted entire issues to black women writers. *Sage*, A Scholarly Journal on Black Women, dedicated their Spring 1985 issue to "Women as Writers," and featured on its cover a portrait of the eighteenth-century writer Phyllis Wheatley, who had for so many generations been neglected or maligned, and about whom Alice Walker had written so eloquently in her essay, "In Search of Our Mothers' Gardens." In the issue was a review essay on *The Color Purple* by Mae Henderson called "The Color Purple: Revisions and Redefinitions." Henderson argued that *The Color Purple* "subverts the traditional Eurocentric mode of the male code which dominates the literary **conventions** of the epistolary novel," and that "Walker has developed a new model for relationships based on new gender roles for men and women." As well the issue included a piece by Alma Freeman, "Zora Neale Hurston and Alice Walker: A Spiritual Kinship," a topic that has become important in Walker scholarship, as well as excerpts from Alice Walker's Journals. In situating Walker within a black female literary tradition, the issue also featured articles on other African-American women writers such as Toni Morrison as well as on West Indian and African women writers. The editors began the issue by referring to the award of the Pulitzer Prize to *The Color Purple* as resulting in a new official phase in Black Women's literary history, although black women have been writing seriously since the eighteenth century. The issue is clearly a tribute to that tradition.

Perhaps the most controversial piece that related *The Color Purple* to a tradition of African-American women writers was Mel Watkins' "Sexism, Racism and Black Women Writers." Published on the front page of *The New York Times Book Review*, the piece received much attention, perhaps because a focus on African-American writers seldom appears in that spot.

Watkins argued that since the publication of Carlene Hatcher Polite's The Flagellants in 1967, "black women writers have tended to focus directly on the **theme** of sometimes bitter antagonism between men and women," and that such a **theme** is "at odds with black literary tradition." Watkins cited *The Color Purple* as having provoked the most heated arguments among blacks but traced the debates it inspired back to Ntozake Shange's *For Colored Girls Who Have Considered Suicide/ When the Rainbow Was Enuf* (1976), and Michelle Wallace's *Black Macho* and the *Myth of the Superwoman* (1979). He cited works by Toni Cade Bambara, Toni Morrison, Gayle Jones as well as

Walker's first novel, *The Third Life of Grange Copeland*, as having contributed to this theme.

ENTER ISHMAEL REED

Watkins also outlined some black men's responses to this **theme**, focusing primarily on comments writer Ishmael Reed had made in the context of *The Color Purple* debate. Reed was not new to controversy. He had been accused by black feminist critics of creating solely derogatory black female characters in his many novels and he had, before the publication of *The Color Purple*, been critical of Morrison and Walker. He argued that black women were being used by white feminists and that writers who portrayed black males in a negative manner were promoted by the white literary establishment. In response to *The Color Purple*, Reed did more than comment; the centerpiece of his novel *Reckless Eyeballing* (1986) is a thinly veiled **parody** of Alice Walker.

Watkins incorporated Reed's comments into the argument that "black writers were particularly wary, until recently, of exposing aspects of inner community life that might reinforce damaging racial stereotypes already proffered by racist antagonists" (he did mention that *Native Son* was an exception to this rule), and that black women writers had chosen to ignore this parameter. He wondered whether this break, in what he thought was a major element in the African-American literary tradition, might not backfire.

AFRICAN-AMERICAN PLURALISM

There were immediate responses to the Watkins piece. Deborah McDowell, a black feminist critic, countered that the African-

American literary tradition had always included varying points of view and that Watkins's conceptualization of the tradition was erroneous and subverted the very idea of literature. Other letters pointed out, as Walker and other writers had, that some black writers are not writing primarily to whites and that the Watkins scenario implied that black literature did not seek truth and was tailored to white ears.

TOPICS IN A NATIONAL DEBATE

The Watkins piece spelled out major points in the debates about *The Color Purple*, which were being held in practically every major black community in the country. Were black writers only to present "positive" views of blacks? Wasn't that another form of stereotyping? To what extent did black women have the freedom to write about sexism within the black community? Had not black women often been negatively portrayed in the predominantly male African-American literary tradition?

WALKER CONTRASTED WITH MORRISON

Mel Watkins's piece appeared on June 15, 1986. By December of that year, the controversy over the novel had not subsided. Fueled by the release of the film *The Color Purple* in December 1985, pieces about Alice Walker continued to be written, some clearly directed at her character. In the Winter 1986 issue of *Black American Literature Forum*, Phillip Royster, Professor of English and Ethnic Studies at Kansas State University, contributed such a piece. It was called "In Search of Our Father's Arms: Alice Walker's Persona of the Alienated Darling." Even the title parodied Walker's essay title "In Search of Our Mother's Gardens." Royster's thesis was that Walker is an "alienated rescuer," who because of a terrible relationship with her father has undertaken a desperate search for father figures. Because of her alienation from her own community, "she has flirted and engaged herself with whites, undoubtedly searching for the acceptance and affirmation that she did not find at home, but she has discovered that they will not relinquish their racism, and so she appears to be searching for a way to return." Royster ended his essay with a quote from Milton Gordon about the marginal man stranded between two cultures of a social order, which describes, he says, a pattern in Walker's life-one of "insecurity, moodiness, hypersensitivity, excessive self-consciousness and nervous strain." Royster's essay also employed a strategy that was beginning to be used in *The Color Purple* debate. He opposed Toni Morrison, a true black writer, to Alice Walker, allegedly an aberrant one.

SOLD OUT?

Royster's piece was not the only negative assault on Walker in the Winter of 1986-87. In a review essay called "Black Victims, Black Villains," in the *New York Review of Books*, January 29, 1987, Darryl Pinckney juxtaposed comments on the novel *The Color Purple*, Ishmael Reed's *Reckless Eyeballing* and the film *The Color Purple*. In his review of the novel *The Color Purple*, Pinckney asserted that *The Color Purple* is closer to Harriet Beecher Stowe than to Zora Neale Hurston and that Walker's works "constitute a body of inspirational literature for the black woman." Pinckney contended that "much of the appeal of *The Color Purple* does not lie in its text, but through representing the black woman's experience in the popular feminist vocabulary, in its power as a symbol of reconciliation between black women and white women in the feminist movement." Like Reed, a novelist he clearly admires, Pinckney implied that Walker had sold out to white feminists. In contrast to his extremely critical review of *The Color Purple*, Pinckney praised Reed's *Reckless Eyeballing* as a novel more in tune with the black literary tradition. He called Reed "one of the most underrated writers in America" and applauded his **parody** of black women writers like Walker. Pinckney concluded his piece with a review of the film *The Color Purple*: "Walker's literary **cliches** meet so well with Spielberg's visual **cliches** because both are derived from the same stereotypes."

WALKER ANSWERS HER CRITICS

Although Alice Walker had been silent about negative black male responses to her novel, she did, in the November 1986 issue of *MS.*, write "a letter to our African-American Friend" called "In the Closet of the Soul." The letter is written in response to a black male friend who asked her how she felt about "the hostile reaction of some people, particularly some black men, to the character of Mister in the book and more particularly in the movie."

Walker responded by underscoring her disappointment that some black men could not empathize with black women's suffering under sexism. She insisted that the black tradition had been always one of fighting all injustices. She went on to point out that both the meek Celie and the brutal Mister are "dreadfully ill" and "manifest their disease according to their culturally derived sex roles and their early impressioned personalities." Walker emphasized that they both grow in the book, by becoming whole, that is "more like each other."

Walker explained how Mister is descended, like many African-Americans, both from slaves and slaveowners, and that his treatment of Celie betrayed his desire to be like the Master, and his ability to love Shug an indication that he is capable of loving himself as black. "We are the Mestizos of North America," Walker declared as she pointed to her own ancestry of black, white, and red strains.

In her discussion, Walker quoted one of her poems, "Family Of," which traced her mixed racial ancestry and to which a black male critic had objected, calling the poem a denial of her blackness. Walker responded to the critic by insisting that it is her black culture which allows her to acknowledge her entire history - that is, her great-great-grandmother was raped by a white man, had a child she couldn't have wanted, and yet nurtured that child. An acknowledgment of all that we are, she insisted, is critical to our development. She ended her letter with the words "In my work and in myself I reflect black people, women and men as I reflect others. One day even the most self-protective ones will look into the mirror I provide and not be afraid."

SCHOLARLY STUDIES

While the debate on *The Color Purple* raged in the media, scholars were publishing analyses of the novel from different perspectives. Elizabeth Fifes wrote on its language in a piece called "Alice Walker, *The Dialect and Letter of The Color Purple*." Barbara Christian and Betty J. Parker, in two different essays for Mari Evans's edition of *Black Women Writers* (1950-80), discussed the novel in relation to all of Walker's work. Christian also published an essay exploring the **theme** of lesbianism in *The Color Purple* and in recent black women's fiction, and an essay on the political context of Walker's three novels, which she saw as a trilogy. In her essay, "The Color Purple Writing to Undo What Writing has Done," Valerie Babb explored the relationship of the oral tradition to writing, while Susan Willis, in her essay, "Alice Walker's Women," analyzed the relationship between the historical process and narrative modes in Walker's three novels. Deborah McDowell used *The Color Purple* as a pivotal novel in her essay "The Changing Same: Generational Connections and Black Women Novelists." McDowell asserted that *The Color Purple* "elevates the folk forms of rural and Southern blacks to the status of art."

JAPANESE ESSAYS ON WALKER

The Color Purple has also received considerable attention from scholars in other parts of the world. It has already been translated into many languages, most recently Chinese. The translator called the work "a very Chinese novel," indicating the international appeal of the novel's themes. And in Japan, scholars are putting together a collection of essays on Walker's works scheduled for publication in Fall 1987.

WALKER'S IMPACT ON AMERICAN LITERATURE

Whatever future scholars' judgment on *The Color Purple* may be, there is no question that it has had an irrevocable effect on American literary history. It has brought to the forefront the richness and power of black folk English; it has emphasized the thematic importance of sexism and racism in the literature, and it has made it clear that African-American women's writing is a significant part of American literature. No longer can literate Americans say that they have never heard of an African-American woman writer.

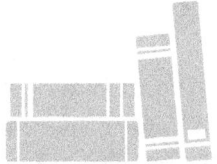

CRITICS RESPOND TO THE FILM VERSION OF THE COLOR PURPLE

The critical response to the film *The Color Purple* should be seen in the context of the history of Hollywood films that have been produced about African-Americans. It is important to remember that while twenty or so Hollywood films have been adapted from African-American men's works, Walker's *The Color Purple* is one of the first novels to be adapted from an African-American woman's novel.

Hollywood has tended to portray black men and women through white stereotypes such as the Mammy and the Sambo. For a discussion of these cinematic stereotypes, students of this subject might want to read studies such as Don Bogle's work, *Mammies, Bucks, Coons and Sambos*, or see a television documentary on stereotyping of blacks in the media called *Ethnic Notions* created by Marlon Riggs. As important as the history of black stereotypes is that there are very few Hollywood films produced about blacks in this country. Any production on this subject matter, then, carries a burden of portraying black life in its entirety, an impossible feat for any one film. The question of audience also affects such productions, since Hollywood films are designed to appeal to a mass audience, most of whom are white Americans. This means that often the material is slanted so as not to offend whites or challenge their historically received images of blacks. In the context of these three factors, films about African-Americans have, of necessity, been controversial and usually unacceptable to the black intellectual and critical world.

The Color Purple was released as a Warner Brothers Production in December 1985. Because of the history of Hollywood films about black novels, and because of the controversial nature of Walker's novel, it is important to discuss how the film became the film that it is.

THE MAKING OF THE COLOR PURPLE

There are many newspaper accounts that describe some aspects of the making of this film. However, three pieces combine much of this information into full accounts: Susan Dworkin's "'The Color Purple' Becomes a Movie," in *MS.*, December 1985; Elena Featherston's "The Making of 'The Color Purple'" in *San Francisco Focus*, December 1985, and the BBC's television documentary on *The Color Purple*. Featherston's piece is particularly interesting since she was on location while the film was being made. Featherston is one of the few African-American women filmmakers. Since 1982, she has been working on a feature film on Walker's life and works. Her film crew shot aspects of the making of *The Color Purple* to be a part of her film on Walker to be released in February 1988.

Both Featherston and Dworkin inform their readers about how Walker made the decision to sell the film rights of the novel. After much soul-searching and consultation with her friends and partner-in-life, Robert Allan, she decided to take this risk because she wanted to get Celie's story out to as many people as possible. Although the novel had sold over a million copies, she knew that the people she wanted to speak to most, not only in this country but also in the rest of the world, did not necessarily read books; but they did go to the movies. Walker also thought that it was necessary to challenge Hollywood's process so that there might be changes in the way it dealt with blacks in the industry. As a result, she agreed to sell the rights of the novel on two conditions: that she would be a consultant to the film and that, apart from the predominantly black cast, half of the people involved in the production of the film would be blacks/women and people of color. This was a rare condition in Hollywood's business dealings with writers.

Another important factor in Walker's decision was that Quincy Jones, the famous black musician and composer, whom she admired, was eager to be one of the film's producers. It was he who asked Steven Spielberg, of *E.T.* fame, to consider directing the film. Because of his obvious box-office appeal, Spielberg's involvement might be helpful in securing financial backing for a controversial film, as *The Color Purple* clearly would be, and to guarantee its distribution in American movie houses.

WHAT WOULD HAPPEN TO HER CHARACTERS

Spielberg was known for slick blockbusters, none of which Walker had then seen. She agreed to sell *Color Purple* film rights to Peter Guber, producer of *Missing*, *Midnight Express*, and *Flashdance* and to accept Spielberg as director of *The Color Purple*, only after having had many conversations with them after seeing *E.T.* Still, Walker had anxiety dreams about what might happen to her characters. Even before the film was released, the fact that Spielberg was its director was a point of controversy among those who had strong feelings about Walker's novel.

Featherston was one of those concerned people. She was somewhat relieved by the casting decisions for the film, that Whoopi Goldberg (Walker's choice) was to play Celie, that Oprah Winfrey, whom Quincy Jones had selected, was to play Sofia, that the seasoned actor Danny Glover was to play Mister. Spielberg had decided to use relatively unknown actors in the casting of the film. Walker had wanted Tina Turner to play the part of Shug but Turner refused saying it was "too close to home" for her. Spielberg selected the unknown Margaret Avery for the part.

But as she traveled to Monroe, South Carolina, where the film was being shot, Featherston was still worried about the choice of Spielberg as director. Her report as well as Walker's comments in *MS.* communicate the trust they both came to feel about Spielberg. Featherston commented: "Watching Spielberg work, his obvious passion, the way he cares about the magic of movie-making and the magic of the human spirit-dispelled any doubts about his grasp of the subtleties of Walker's work." Walker agreed. In her interview with BBC as well as in Dworkin's article for *MS.*, she declared "What impressed me most about that meeting [with Spielberg] was Steven's absolute grasp of the essentials of the book, the feeling, the spirit."

EMPHASIS ON "MISTER"

In the *MS.* article, Walker did allow that there were real differences between the novel and the rushes of the film. Considering audience response, Spielberg had muted "the lesbian theme," and did not focus on the woman-centered world of the Memphis scenes in the novel. The film emphasized Mister in ways that the novel had not, partly because of Danny Glover's powerful screen presence. Still, Walker believed the film preserved the strength and power of the women's relationship in the novel.

Walker had not written the script for the movie. She had tried but found that she could not give birth to Celie's story twice. Instead Menno Meyes, a Dutchman by birth, wrote the movie's script, which Walker approved. Walker also worked as a consultant in the film. "At every moment," Jones stated, "Alice was considered the last word."

Walker affected greatly one aspect of the film-its setting. Like many others, Spielberg thought the physical environment of *The Color Purple* was poverty-stricken. In the BBC production, Walker discussed how she helped the film crew on the issue of the class to which her characters belonged - that they were landowners who lived in a relatively comfortable house with good furnishings. She showed them pictures of Spelman graduates, and of the black middle-class in Georgia at the turn of the century, who dressed well and indulged in fine lace. Ironically, this is one area of the film that has been criticized, for reviewers, like readers of the novel, came to this work with the assumption that all Southern blacks were desperately poor.

In addition to the accounts of the making of *The Color Purple*, Warner Brothers' prepublicity affected its reception. Possibly because it wanted to dispel fears about the film's social message and because it wanted to appeal to a holiday audience consisting primarily of whites, Warner Brothers billed *The Color Purple* as a film "about the human experience," rather than about the "black experience or the black experience," Walker's comments on the phrase "the human experience" are interesting in the context of the film's prepublicity. When Elena Featherston asked her if, "As a black writer, do you feel you write about the human a experience," Walker replied, "if you go deeply into yourself, into your idiom it's inevitable then that you come upon other people ... Black women have different angle from which to write ... Black women have to look out and through all those people who have traditionally been on top of them: the black man, the white woman, the white man. This creates a different way of looking at reality."

THE FILM GENERATES CONTROVERSY

Benefit premieres of the film *The Color Purple* were held in major American cities, New York City, Los Angeles, San Francisco. Even before its release, the film generated controversy. Members of a group in Los Angeles called The Coalition Against Black Exploitation picketed the Los Angeles premiere and charged that the film would present negative images of the black family. At the same time, Gene Shallit of the Today Show, who had previewed the film, praised it with the highly publishable comment "that it should be against the law not to see it."

In her review for the San Francisco paper, *Coming Up*, Kim Corsaro reported Walker's comments at the San Francisco premiere, which was a benefit for the Women's Building and the School of Dramatic Arts. Speaking to an audience many of whom had loved the book, Walker said that the first time she saw the film, she didn't like it and went into mourning for a week. But after she had seen it a second time she loved it as a movie that was quite separate from her novel. Corsaro too was disappointed with the film although her second viewing of it did not result in her loving it.

"SEPARATE THE NOVEL FROM THE MOVIE"

Robert Taylor, movie reviewer for the *Oakland Tribune*, who assessed the film the day after the San Francisco premiere, also advised audiences to separate the novel from the movie. "Alice Walker's admirers may have their own ideas about a film version of *The Color Purple*. But this is not a movie for readers of Pulitzer Prize novels. It is Spielberg's kind of filmmaking for a mass audience - the heightened melodrama, grand gestures, romantic music and eventually ... a joyous uplifting message."

UPLIFTING?

Some reviewers did not think the movie was uplifting. In particular, most black male reviewers were incensed by the movie, as they had been by the book. In his compilation of reviews of *The Color Purple* for *Black Film Review*, March 1986, David Nicholsen outlined the many responses to the movie. Nicholsen's title "From Coast to Coast Purple Aroused Passions" succinctly communicated how controversial the film had become. He reported that there were public forums on *The Color Purple* from Howard University in Washington, D.C., to the University of California, Berkeley, and in black communities all over the country. Even columnists "who didn't regularly review movies got into the act."

Nicholsen's overview revealed three general positions that reviewers took: There were critics who had seen the novel as an attack on black men and were even more incensed by Spielberg's treatment. There were critics who had admired the novel and felt that Spielberg distorted and homogenized it. There were critics who were ambivalent about the film's merits but were pleased that it had been made.

Black male reviewers, as a group, were upset by the film's portrayal of black men. Perhaps the most vociferous of these was Tony Brown, who hosts a national television show, Tony Brown's Journal, and writes columns for black newspapers across the country. Brown admitted that he had not seen the movie nor did he intend to. For him *The Color Purple* was part of the racist ideological attacks on black men for which this country was known. Other black male critics agreed: William Hamlin of the *Oakland Post* in a review called "'The Color Purple': Apartheid's Orgy of Black Male Hatred" stated: "Had Reagan, Botha and/or Hitler corroborated to find a tool that would be injurious to the already fragile relationship between black men and women, they could not have done better than '*The Color Purple*.'" *The Muslim Paper* featured an article whose title summed up the anger this group of reviewers expressed. Called "Purple Poison Pulsing through the Community," it focused not only on the portrayal of men in the film, but also on the emphasis on lesbianism as one woman's means to liberation, a **theme** that the film barely approached.

ONE-SIDED PORTRAYAL OF "MISTER"?

Black male reviewers were not the only ones to object to Spielberg's portrayal of Mister. Many commented that Danny Glover's Mister dominated the screen in such a way that the film seemed to be more his than Celie's. In her review, "In Adapting the Film, Spielberg Left Out Too Much," the black woman critic Rita B. Dandridge complained that Spielberg did not show the development of Mister from a bully to a man who becomes friends with Celie. Nor, she continued, "did Spielberg sufficiently show the problems that Mister faces in the novel: a meddling, dominating father, stuck with wives he doesn't want, annoyed by his no-good children and rejected by Shug Avery, the lover he cannot possess." As a result of Spielberg's one-sided portrayal of Mister, Dandridge concluded, some black men had boycotted the film.

Practically all black reviewers responded to the way Spielberg turned tragic or ironic events of the novel which focused on racism into pieces of slapstick humor. They were particularly incensed by his portrayal of Miss Millie and his omission of the mayor's importance as well as the sheriff's involvement in Sofia's tragedy. Most concluded that Spielberg was not familiar with the subject matter of *The Color Purple*, which was the film's downfall. Marti Wilson in *Black Film Review* put it this way: "Spielberg should be knighted as Hollywood's most intrepid foreign film director of the year. But while he may be lauded for taking on this project with such unfamiliar material, that very fact becomes the film's major downfall.... His film falls right in with the cinematic tradition of handling blacks as clowns who cannot be taken seriously."

Like Marti Wilson, many women reviewers were not happy with the film but for somewhat different reasons than black male reviewers. Michelle Wallace, in her review for the *Village Voice*, called "What's Wrong with This Picture," accused Spielberg of juggling "film **cliches** and racial stereotypes fast and loose, until all signs of a black feminist agenda are banished." Rita B. Dandridge pointed out that Walker's rendition of challenging sex-defined work roles through the characters of Harpo and Sofia is transformed by Spielberg into the minstrel images of Sapphire and Kingfish of the infamous Amos and Andy series. In her review for *Sojourner*, Monica Raymond stated that: "Though black women are still at the center of the movie, though ostensibly it still focuses on the love between sisters both of heart and of blood, these themes have been emptied, made acceptable, controlled. It's not the color purple we notice so much as the heavy hand of the filmmaker." And Kim Corsaro in her review for *Coming Up* was disappointed that the movie chose "not to develop the love between Celie and Shug as the lesbian relationship it is in the novel."

SUBVERSIVE ASPECTS DISREGARDED?

Film journal reviewers were also ambivalent about the merits of the film. In her review for *Jump Out*, called "The Color Purple: Community of Women," Sara Halprin described her love for the novel. She thought, as a white outsider, that the film depicted black culture "in terms of community, variety, richness and range of character and image, and in terms of deep, wide support systems," but objected to "the film's shying away from the lesbian theme," its avoidance of "spirituality and changed roles for men," and that "the film shows Shug Avery's entire character as motivated by her problematic relationship with her father." Halprin concluded: "In short, all the elements of the novel which are most subversive in terms of sexual, rather than race or class-conceived politics, have become totally disregarded or changed in the film."

Although most reviewers were hostile or ambivalent, some did think it was important and worthwhile. Dorothy Gilliam, a black columnist for *The Washington Post*, called *The Color Purple* "a film about the purity and depth of love," and that it should be used as a springboard to address issues of sexism which do exist in African-American culture. Luisah Teish, a well-known African-American woman writer, praised the film as "refreshing, because there is not one murder in it." She asked "What are the choices for a writer or performer? To put out flat material that has no content, does not identify any problems, and therefore does not heal any wounds?"

Teish's response to the film echoed one reason why Walker decided to let her novel be made into a film. In an interview in Sojourner, she said "A writer like me, who writes for a lot of people who don't read, has to think of visual things, ways of reaching them. And even if the story is not entirely my vision when it gets to the screen, I think that just because of what I have given to it, it will be progressive enough for people to see some necessary reflections of themselves."

NOMINATED FOR ELEVEN OSCARS

The film *The Color Purple* certainly exposed the contradictions black writers and actors faced in getting their material out to the general public and brought to a head seemingly unsurmountable obstacles that blacks faced in the American cultural arena. Even as reviewers debated the merits of the film, it was nominated for eleven Oscars, but won none. The NAACP chapter in Los Angeles, who had vociferously protested the film, then charged the Motion Picture Academy with racism. In *Cineaste*, Karen Jaehne wrote a piece called "The Final Word," which asked basic questions about the reactions the film had generated. She pointed out that Spielberg "was not the only cook in the kitchen." "Walker had granted Quincy Jones a lion's share of control over the film and had made herself available.... Whose misinterpretation then is to be blamed for the film's distorted panorama of Southern blacks?" Jaehne asks whether "it is realistic of blacks to expect Hollywood to make black films as a public relations tool? ... Would the independent production route have served the work better or doomed it to burial among special interest groups? ... Will the black community support its own cinema?"

Jaehne was proposing questions about the very nature of Hollywood films and about black artists' dilemmas in getting out their message in an industry designed for profit rather than artistic integrity. There are questions, no doubt, confronting the scholars who will be analyzing the film. *The Color Purple.* In the meantime, the film has created discussion about the issues Walker addressed in her work to an extent that even her Pulitzer Prize novel was not able to do.

As Jaehne was writing her "final word," *The Color Purple* was still being "reviewed" by moviegoers who expressed a variety of opinions through letters and their involvement in talk shows such as Tony Brown's Journal and The Phil Donahue Show. Clearly, many people loved the movie for the very cinematic qualities critics had decried-its sentimentality and emotionalism, its grand color and music. Others emphasized the view that the film was an attack on black men. Some felt that even the brief scene between Shug and Celie that "smacked of lesbianism" was too much. Many were thrilled by the focus on black women in the film. As time passes and tempers cool, one thing is certain. Many people who never had read serious literature did read the novel *The Color Purple* after they'd seen the film.

THE THIRD LIFE OF GRANGE COPELAND

Walker's first novel traces three generations of a Southern sharecropping family, the Copelands. Its time span, like that of many African-American women's novels, is from the 1920s to the 1950s. The central **theme** of the novel is the tension between systematic societal oppression which attempts to destroy the individual will, and the possibility than an individual can have any personal responsibility under such extreme social conditions. This **theme**, implicit in all protest novels, is brought to the fore in this book.

Walker demonstrates her **theme** through a graphic portrayal of the effects of the Southern racist system and the false gender definitions on the black family. The Copeland men have no access to the definition of maleness in their society - that of power. They vent their anger and frustration on their wives, who have been socialized to the definition of woman as compliant and subordinate childbearers. The result is a family that almost destroys itself.

Walker describes the first life of Grange Copeland as daily toil, and submission to the white boss man, interrupted only by drunken bouts with Josie, the local whore, assaults on his wife, and churchgoing. Grange hates himself for being so powerless that he has nothing to give to his son Brownfield. Finally he deserts his family and goes North, the traditional route of escape for the runaway slave. His wife Margaret kills her newborn baby and commits suicide, leaving their adolescent son to fend for himself.

MALE PATTERN REPEATED

Brownfield too decides to go North but on his way meets Mem, a schoolteacher whom he marries. He resolves to change the life his father had to leave. But despite hard work and his love for Mem, he ends up, like his father, in debt to the white boss man. He repeats his father's pattern, beats his wife, neglects his children, and lives in despair. Mem attempts to change their life by working and finding a house in the town. But Brownfield resents her show of strength, which he interprets as an attack on his manhood. Mem must give up her house when she becomes pregnant again. Finally, Brownfield kills her on Christmas Eve-leaving his children to fend for themselves. But this time, there is a change in the pattern. A disillusioned Grange returns from the North where he found he was not only oppressed but invisible. He determines to bring up his granddaughter Ruth, marries Josie, and buys a farm with her money.

Grange's third life fills the second half of the novel, as he teaches Ruth about life, the land, and her people. In contrast to the bleakness of the first half of the book, this section is warm, filled with periods of love. But Grange must live out the results of the old pattern, the despair and anger of the son he never fathered. Despite Grange's warnings to Brownfield that "white folks ain't gods," and "we do have our own souls, don't we?" Brownfield attempts to destroy his father. While he is in jail, he plots with Josie and enlists the racist judicial system to bring his father down. At the end of the novel, police kill Grange. Nevertheless, Ruth has grown up with some understanding of her history and Civil Rights workers are entering the area, an indication that there is hope for her and for the survival of this family.

RURAL VERSUS URBAN RESISTANCE

In the novel, social change cannot occur without personal change. It is Grange's love for his granddaughter that makes it possible for him to have the will to challenge the system. Too, in this novel, change occurs not in the North but in the South among "ordinary" peasants, a point of view that was distinct in 1970 when most African-American writers focused on resistance in urban areas.

Like *Once*, *The Third Life of Grange Copeland* is written in a series of short units. Motifs are consciously arranged in patterns of repetition and variation. For example, one chapter is a detailed description of Grange's week that is repeated with some variations many chapters later when Walker gives us a detailed description of Brownfield's life. In this novel, we begin to see Walker's experimentation with the techniques of quilting.

The Third Life of Grange Copeland also relates to poems Walker is writing at the time, particularly poems about Southern black peasant women and men, which appear in *Revolutionary Petunias*, the volume of poetry she later published in 1973. Grange Copeland focuses on motherhood as a source of strength but also of extreme restrictions for women, a central **theme** in *Meridian*. Mem Copeland is an example of the first type of black woman, the physically and psychologically abused woman that Walker would write about in *In Love & Trouble* and later in

The Color Purple. But unlike Celie, Mem cannot liberate herself for she is isolated in her struggle and does not understand the dimensions of her society. *The Third Life* also features the growing up of Ruth, a young Southern girl, and what she learns about what it is to be a woman, a focal **theme** in Walker's other two novels.

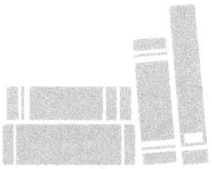

IN LOVE & TROUBLE: STORIES OF BLACK WOMEN

Walker's first collection of short stories includes pieces begun in her adolescence as well as stories about the effects of the Civil Rights Movement on Southern life. In an interview, she tells us that for years she carried around a story about interracial love. That piece became "The Child Who Favored Daughter," a lyrical and violent story about a black father who discovers his daughter loves a white man, and about the daughter who refuses to deny her love. Another story in this volume, "To Hell with Dying," which is about a nurturing relationship between an old southern black man and a young girl who goes to a white school in the North, was written when Walker was in college. One story, "The African Nun," which is about the conflicts of religion and cultures, seems to be related to her experiences in Africa.

In Love & Trouble consists of thirteen stories, eleven of which are told from the point of view of Southern women, as Walker insists on giving voice to her sisters. Few volumes are written from the point of view of black Southern women. This is one of the first. In this volume, there are stories about various sorts of Southern women: of Roselily, a peasant woman who wonders during her marriage ceremony to a Northern Muslim whether she is exchanging one yoke for another; of Mryna, a middle-class woman whose husband wants her to wear frilly dresses, stay at home, have babies, and not write stories. There are stories about older women, e.g., the old woman in "The Welcome Table" who opposes the racist system by entering a white church, and about Hannah Kemhuff in "The Revenge of Hannah Kemhuff," who uses voodoo to wreak revenge on the white woman who had destroyed her family. There are stories about taboo subjects such as interracial love in "The Child Who Favored Daughter," and a student/teacher love relationship in "We Drink the Wine in France." There are stories about black women's creativity, quilting in "Everyday Use," folk medicine in "Strong Horse Tea." And there are stories about the relationship between young girls and the old as in "To Hell with Dying."

In most of these stories, the women, often against their own conscious will, oppose the **conventions** of relations in the South, either in their own minds, through words, or in action. Walker situates her stories with an epigraph to the volume, a quote from Rainer Maria Rilke, which states that every living thing spontaneously opposes that which restricts its natural growth. Society, even the women **protagonists** themselves, might call their words, actions, thoughts, madness, since they result in trouble, violence, even death. But Walker's writing shows us that these women act naturally, that their subversive thoughts, words, and actions are healthy in that they resist the sexist and racist traditions which restrict them.

FORM AND RITUAL

In these stories, Walker experiments with forms, derived from women's traditions. "Roselily" is written in the form of a marriage ceremony, "Really, Doesn't Crime Pay," as a series of Mryna's diary entries, a form similar to Celie's letters in *The Color Purple*. Often, ritual is the kernel of a story's form: the contrast of African chant and Christian chant in "The African Nun," the conjugation of verbs in "We Drink the Wine in France."

In Love & Trouble is a controversial volume that clearly indicates there is sexism in the black community, a point of view not often written about in 1973. Some of these stories reiterate **themes** Walker would develop further in later works. She questions in "Roselily" and "My Sweet Jerome" whether black nationalist ideology will free black women, a **theme** further developed in *Meridian*. She asks, as well, whether middle-class status is not restrictive for women, a **theme** in *Meridian* as well as *The Color Purple*. The concept of black patriarchy so compellingly portrayed in "The Child Who Favored Daughter" takes on wider dimensions in *The Color Purple*.

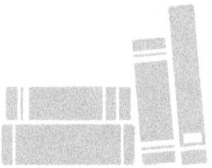

REVOLUTIONARY PETUNIAS AND OTHER POEMS

Like *In Love & Trouble, Revolutionary Petunias* is concerned with false conventions, this time of "The Southern Revolution" of the 1960s. In these poems, Walker celebrates those folk who are open to change within themselves as well as in society, a process that sometimes runs counter to the **conventions** of revolutionary ideologues. Like Meridian in Walker's next novel, those who do not hold to such **conventions** are often seen as outcasts. Yet, it is these wayward folk who are often the ones that effect lasting change. The central **theme** in this volume, as in all of Walker's works, is the relationship between the difficult process of personal change and societal change. As is often the case, Walker's poetry emphasizes the personal aspect of that relationship.

"... NOT THE FIRST TO FIGHT ..."

This volume consists of five movements, each one indicating a stage in the personal journey towards wholeness. The first movement, "In These Dissenting Times," focuses on the importance of ordinary folk who precede us as the foundation of any meaningful change. At a time when the revolutionaries of the 1960s tended to disregard their forebears as ineffectual or bourgeois, Walker reminds us of the women of her mother's generation, "Husky of voice - Stout of/ Step/ With fists as well as/ Hands," and that "we/ are not the first to suffer, rebel,/ fight, love and die."

BEAUTY AND REVOLUTION

In the second movement, "*Revolutionary Petunias* - The Living Through," she combines into one symbol two unlikely concepts, that of the petunia, an ordinary yet beautiful flower, and revolution, that much overused term for change. During this period, "revolutionaries" sometimes characterized the need for beauty in life as a trivial matter, and in spite of their commitment to the masses expressed contempt for "backward" ordinary folk who had not read the right books. Yet, it is those ordinary folk, Walker contends, who are the changers of society and who, like her mother, understand the need for beauty in life. Because many ideologues proclaimed that "poems of/ love and flowers are/ a luxury the Revolution/ cannot afford," many people were labeled "incorrect" and were castigated or ignored. Poems in this movement, like "Outcast," and "Expect Nothing," explore the feelings of being in such a position.

"CRUCIFIXATION"

The third movement, "Crucifixation" dwells on the suffering of those who refuse to submit to false **conventions** and insist, like Meridian, "on allowing an idea ... to penetrate [their] life." But some come through this crucifixation to the fourth stage, "Mysteries ... the Living Beyond." There are many love poems in this movement, marked by serenity and personal renewal.

PETUNIA AS SYMBOL

The last movement is a single short poem, "The Nature of this Flower Is to Bloom." For Walker, this is what revolution is about - the creation of conditions that allow us all to bloom as she reiterates the oneness of life at the center of her philosophy. The petunia is symbolic of the commonness, beauty, and exuberance of those committed to change.

Like the poems of *Once*, most poems in this volume are succinct; yet in this second collection of poetry, one can hear Walker's growth as a poet. There is more authority in her voice as she carefully selects few yet compelling images in poems that are as lyrical as they are thoughtful.

Revolutionary Petunias could be seen as the poetry companion to the short-story collection, *In Love & Trouble*, and as well a precursor to her novel about "The Southern Revolution" published in 1976. There are poems such as "Outcast" and "Eagle Rock" that relate directly to sections in *Meridian*. There are poems, like "Revolutionary Petunias" (a **ballad** of an ordinary Southern woman, known for her petunias, who kills the white man who murdered her son), which remind us of the old woman in "The Welcome Table" of *In Love & Trouble*. Particularly the first segment of this volume looks back to *The Third Life of Grange Copeland*, while the poem "Burial," about Walker's grandmother Rachel, provides a model for Celie in *The Color Purple*. As well the use of flowers, a motif throughout *In Love & Trouble* and the essay "In Search of Our Mothers' Gardens," is the central image of *Revolutionary Petunias*. This volume is pivotal in Walker's opus.

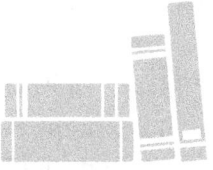

MERIDIAN

Walker's second novel, *Meridian*, is, in one sense, a continuation of her first. The novel is set primarily during the period of the Civil Rights Movement, which is foreshadowed at the end of *The Third Life of Grange Copeland*. Like that first novel, *Meridian* traces the generations of a black Southern family, but this time through the mothers rather than the fathers. In this innovative work, Walker tells us stories about black Southern culture through a more imaginative nonlinear use of quilting than the patchwork quilting of Grange Copeland. Although Grange Copeland is concerned with the way racism and patriarchy affect black fathers, *Meridian* explores these ideologies' effects on black mothers. *Meridian* is both a celebration of black mothers and a critique of the ideology of motherhood.

The plot centers on Meridian Hill, an ordinary lower middle-class woman, who becomes pregnant in the 1950s when she is in high school, who marries, has a son and then gives up that son, as mothers had to, for only virgins could become students. She is intensely involved in the Civil Rights Movement while she is at Saxon College, a ladylike school for black girls. There she becomes involved with Truman Held, a Civil Rights activist from the North. She becomes pregnant, has an abortion but does not tell Truman, who is infatuated with Lynne, a white woman activist from the North. These three,

Meridian, Truman, and Lynne, help to create the triumphs and contradictions of the movement even as they are changed by it. Obsessed by her guilt that she is an unworthy mother and concerned with the movement's ideological turn towards violence, Meridian goes on a pilgrimage through the South. In that journey she becomes more than a biological mother as she nurtures all life-for Walker an essential quality of a revolutionary. It is her intense involvement with the folk, and her understanding of her maternal ancestors, their suffering, shame, and creativity that are Meridian's guides to the health she seeks.

ASCENDING CIRCLES

Although this may be a synopsis of the novel, this description is not the way a reader experiences *Meridian*. The novel begins in the 1970s, moves back to the 1960s, further back in time through Meridian's mother to her grandmothers, and then forward in time to the 1970s. Only the last part of the novel moves beyond the time at which it begins as Walker constructs a pattern of revolution, going backwards in order to come forward beyond one's initial point, in a series of ascending circles, the meaning of the word meridian. In arranging the time sequences, Walker allows us to hear the mind-voices of Meridian, Lynne, and Truman.

This novel is constructed as a crazy quilt in which certain motifs are reiterated. There are two major groups: music as a basic concept of harmony and wholeness; and guilt, the basic concept of fragmentation, alienation, violence. Walker uses these two concepts in the coalescing of motifs of which the many short sections of the novel construct a whole. Some motifs are: Indians, as the embodiment of the unity of Nature even as they are peoples almost destroyed by violent conquest; children, as the embodiment of the future but also as the beings most vulnerable to violence in the society; mothers, as sanctified in the society even as they are punished for being mothers; sexuality, as a source of connectedness but also as an oppressive force for women. The motifs that Walker explores are natural and good and yet are assaulted by societal violence, by the ideologies of sexism, racism, exploitation.

As Walker traces the nature of the Civil Rights Movement through Meridian, Lynne, and Truman, she shows how it is necessarily affected by the very societal violation it opposes, since it is composed of persons who have internalized these violations. And that change comes through the interrelationship of personal and social transformation. One cannot achieve lasting personal transformation unless the society changes and the society cannot change unless individuals seek personal change.

STORIES WITHIN THE STORY

Meridian is also a novel composed of stories, one of Walker's literary characteristics. Woven into the stories of the three main characters are anecdotes about other people's lives: folk tales such as the story of the slave Louvenia, whose clipped-out tongue is the root of the Magic Tree, Sojourner; as well as contemporary tales such as the story of the wild child and the nationally viewed funeral of Martin Luther King, Jr. The juxtaposition of these stories within a story is one means by which Walker demonstrates the relationship between folk history and contemporary mores.

Meridian is a novel of personal and political struggle, and it is one of the few American novels about a national social movement. At the crux of the many questions it poses is the relationship of violence to social change. It asks the question, when is revolutionary murder not murder? How does one effect change without violating the very ideas one wishes to nourish? And it presents the experience of mothering as a critical source from which those intent on social change can learn.

Meridian is an extensive elaboration of **themes** and techniques Walker had explored in the seventies: her focus on black Southern tradition, on black women's history and creativity, her experimentation with the technique of quilting and with history as a means of creating depth in a work of art. The novel also looks forward to other works for it brings up many issues that Walker would write about in the eighties, e.g. the issue of abortion in "The Abortion" and of interracial rape in "Advancing Luna." And *Meridian*'s focus on the destruction of the land is a central **theme** in her more recent publication, *Horses Make the Landscape Look More Beautiful*.

Meridian is Walker's novel of struggle. Her works after this novel exude confidence about the positive effects social movements such as the Civil Rights Movement and the Women's Movement can have on society and particularly on black women's lives. Her next three publications resound with the **theme** of one of these book titles - that *You Can't Keep a Good Woman Down*.

GOOD NIGHT WILLIE LEE, I'LL SEE YOU IN THE MORNING

Walker's third collection of poetry takes its title from her mother's farewell words to her father at his funeral. These words are the frame for a volume whose major **theme** is the connections between love relationships and lasting change. The volume is divided into five sections moving from a night of loss to a morning of hope. Through this journey Walker demystifies love as a disease and redefines it as health.

The volume begins with a poem about love as disease: "Did This Happen to Your Mother, Did Your Sister Throw Up a Lot?" We suffer with the poet through a period of love as a giving up of selfhood until she is shown a way back to herself by other women; her mother, friends, and writers from the past, like Zora Neale Hurston. The poem "On Stripping Bark From Myself," one of Walker's finest, is a declaration of selfhood. She declares: "I find my own/ small person/ a standing self/ against the world/ an equality of wills/ I finally understand." That declaration enables her to ask questions about the connections between intimate relationships and the love that inspires the struggle for social change. In the process, the poet learns, like her mother, that it is the forgiveness of oneself and of others which leads to a love without possessiveness or fear.

Like *Revolutionary Petunias*, the poems in this volume are usually succinct, spare, a notable exception being the long poem "Early Losses," which traces personal and social loss. A large part of this poem dramatizes the loss of home and the scars that resulted from African-Americans' capture from Africa and their enslavement in America, an indication of Walker's focus on Africa so evident in *The Color Purple*. There are many love poems in *Good Night Willie Lee, I'll See You in the Morning* as there are in *Revolutionary Petunias*. But while Walker's second collection stresses a forbidden love, the love poems in her third collection exude an air of confidence about the poet's ability to cherish herself as the basis for loving others.

Some of the poems point to **themes** Walker was then exploring in short stories as well as in *The Color Purple*, the novel she would publish a few years later. That women must love themselves in order to be healthy, as contrasted with the many societal restrictions which insist on their role as a giving up of the self, is focal in *Good Night Willie Lee, I'll See You in the Morning* as well as in her next collection of short stories, *You Can't Keep a Good Woman Down*. This **theme** develops into an exploration of how genuine love of others is dependent on self-love, and like *The Color Purple*, these themes are framed by the love within a family. *Good Night Willie Lee* also points back to *Meridian*, for it is the forgiveness of self and of others which Meridian learns at the end of the novel, an indication that she is on her way to spiritual health. By using the images of disease and health in relation to love, Walker explores how a society's definition of love is an indication of its values.

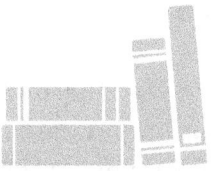

YOU CAN'T KEEP A GOOD WOMAN DOWN

Like Good Night Willie Lee, Walker's second collection of short stories is thematically unified by the concept that intimate relationships are not only personal, they are political. The title *You Can't Keep a Good Woman Down*, is taken from a female blues song of that name and is a pointed indication of the confidence so characteristic of this period of Walker's work.

Many of these stories are about issues previously considered too topical for fiction: abortion, pornography, sadomasochism, interracial rape. That this collection focuses on such issues indicates the tremendous impact the Black Civil Right's and Women's Movements have had on American society. A mere fifteen years before, most of these topics would not have been written about from the point of view of a black woman. Many of these stories are distinctively erotic, in contrast to Walker's previous work. Throughout the collection, she delves into aspects of sexuality, and how our internalized values about it restrict women.

The tone and technique of this collection are contemporary. Many of the black women **protagonists** in these stories have traveled, even from one continent to another; many are economically independent, even famous. They are testing the freedom that their social and spatial mobility indicate, freedoms which they have won during the last few decades, but which they often find they still cannot actualize without fighting for them. Unlike the women in *In Love & Trouble*, however, these women are conscious of their right to fulfillment, and attempt to achieve it, whatever the obstacles. It is in this collection that Walker first uses the term "womanist." The volume is full of women who define themselves as womanists or who are attempting to achieve that goal.

PROCESS VERSUS PRODUCT

In keeping with the contemporary tone, the form of many of these stories is that of a story in process, in keeping with the feminist idea that process, rather than completed product, is akin to woman's experience. So "Advancing Luna," a story about a black woman's view of interracial rape, has three endings and Walker, the writer, does what a twentieth-century writer is not supposed to do. She enters the narrative and speaks as herself. Another story, "The Letter," is written in the form of a letter from a black woman to a white woman about sadomasochism, and "1955," the story of the blues singer, Gracie Mae Stills, is written entirely as diary entries. "Coming Apart," a story about a husband and wife's struggle over the pornography magazines he is addicted to, is framed by the wife's reading to the husband black-womanist essays on this issue.

You Can't Keep a Good Woman Down is related to Walker's past work in that it includes stories like "A Sudden Trip Home in the Spring" in which a young black woman is trying to understand her relationship to her Southern family, particularly her difficult father who has just died. The volume also looks forward to *The Color Purple*, particularly in its experimentation with the letter form and with the development of a female blues singer as a major character. This volume is a graphic demonstration of how pivotal issues of women's sexuality are to Walker's work at this time, issues that characterize her most famous work, *The Color Purple*.

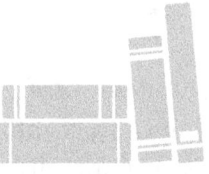

ONCE

The poems in *Once* touch on many subjects: growing up in the South, Civil Rights activity, images of Africa, love and suicide. These subjects reflect Walker's childhood, her education, and her travels to Africa and Europe. A common voice unites the poems; it is the voice of a person who asks difficult questions about life and who is not afraid of contradiction. In Africa, as well as in the American South, the poet sees both beauty and pain. For example, in the poem "South: the name of Home," there are images like "a broken bottle/ held negligently; in a racist/ fist," as well as "the smell of one magnolia," which "sends [the poet's] heart running through the swamp."

Once is an early indication that Walker prefers succinct, direct language and short units that have been honed down to the core. She values the grace that comes from spareness, a quality that marks the style of all of her works.

In this volume, many poems reverberate with work she has yet to write. Poems like "Once" and "Chic Freedom Song," which are about Civil Rights demonstrations, relate to sections of Meridian. "**Ballad** of the Browngirl" treats the **theme** of interracial love, as does one of the first short stories

Walker wrote, "The Child Who Favored Daughter," which was published in *In Love & Trouble*. And in *Once*, there are poems like "African Images" that relate to the Nettie section of *The Color Purple*.

ALICE WALKER

WALKER AFTER THE COLOR PURPLE

Despite the flurry of attention that drained her energy when she received the Pulitzer, Alice Walker has continued to be a prolific writer and an involved activist. She has done benefit readings for political causes such as the anti-apartheid movement and the anti-nuclear movement, issues which she has also written about. Her press, Wild Trees Press, has released four publications: J. California Cooper's *A Piece of Mine: Stories*, Jo Anne Brasil's novel *Billy's Bar-B-Que*, Charlotte Mendez's novel *Condor and Hummingbird*, and Septima Clark's biography as told to Cynthia Brown, *Ready From Within*. Since 1982, Walker has also published two books.

IN SEARCH OF OUR MOTHERS' GARDENS: WOMANIST PROSE (1983)

This volume is a collection of essays Walker wrote during the last twenty years. It charts her growth and indicates the important influences on her life and work. As such, it is invaluable to anyone interested in Walker's works, for through the essay form she elaborates upon ideas that are central to her poetry, short stories, novels. The essay form is part of Walker's artistic process and one means by which she communicates the ideas that are important to her.

Included in this volume are classic essays that outline Walker's search for literary models such as "Saving the Life That Is Your Own," and "In Search of Our Mothers' Gardens;" book reviews on other writers who have influenced her; essays about her own process like "Writing *The Color Purple*," political speeches she has made such as "Only Justice Can Stop a Curse."

As in her other writings, Walker's voice is in her essays unmistakably her own-lucid, spare language, anecdotes that make clear the relationship between life and intellectual concepts, experimentation with different forms within the traditional essay form all characterize this volume. As its title indicates, this collection delineates Walker's term womanism and is, in many ways, the story of how she has come to be a womanist.

HORSES MAKE THE LANDSCAPE LOOK MORE BEAUTIFUL: POEMS (1984)

This collection of poetry takes its name from the words of Lame Deer, the Native American Seer who tells us that one thing the white man brought his people, in return for which he almost can forgive them for bringing whiskey, is the horse, because "horses make the landscape look more beautiful." This epigraph sets the tone for a volume that is very much about the sacredness of the land. The volume is also introduced by Walker's poem "Family Of" in which she commemorates the various racial aspects of her ancestry. The poem ends: "Rest. In Peace/ in me/ the meaning/ of our lives/ is still/ unfolding/ Rest." This volume's epigraph and introduction signal its two focal **themes** which are intertwined: the relationship between the various strands of Walker's ancestry and the land.

There are poems in this collection about personal love, such as Walker's memory of her father. There are poems about apartheid and colonialism, where greed destroys human beings and violates Nature. And there are poems specifically about the sacredness of the earth and its possible destruction. Many of the poems in this volume invoke the Spirit as embodied in the image of the color purple.

As is true of most of Walker's work, these poems are succinct, direct, graceful. And as always she experiments with different forms, e.g., the song and the chant. The longest poem in *Horses*, "These Days," uses the refrain "Surely the earth can be saved for - ", as Walker uses in that space the name of one of her friends. The poem ends "Surely the earth can be saved for us," an indication that Walker is increasingly concerned about whether we will destroy the earth. This **theme** may very well be the major focus of her next work.

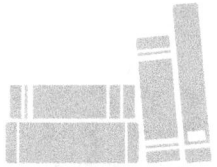

IDEAS FOR PAPERS, DISCUSSIONS, AND ORAL REPORTS

WALKER IN THE EPISTOLARY TRADITION.

The Color Purple is one of the greatest examples of the epistolary novel, i.e., a novel developed in a series of letters. Some advantages of the epistolary format are: it allows the novelist to reveal the main character's private feelings while advancing the action; it requires that the reader visualize the action from the point of view of a character who reflects on events and tries to interpret them for specific purposes; it provides the author with a natural way to shift the point of view as the characters answer each other's letters.

In the light of these advantages about the epistolary format, compare Walker's use of it with that of Samuel Richardson in *Pamela* (1740) or *Clarissa* (1748), or Johann Wolfgang von Goethe in *The Sorrows of Young Werther* (1774).

WALKER'S COMPLEX OF PLOTS

Report on *The Color Purple* as a complex structure of plots (Celie's life in America, Nettie's in America and Africa) and several subplots. (Shug's many loves; Harpo's, Sofia's, and Connie's complicated lives).

How is each plot or subplot resolved? How do they interrelate? Interact? Contrast with each other? Affect each other? To what extent is the turning point (Celie's inheritance) an artificial device to rescue the characters, a **deus ex machina** ending?

PARALLEL PLOTS: WALKER AND BENNETT

Walker's use of parallel plots in *The Color Purple* resembles Arnold Bennett's in *The Old Wives' Tale*. In Walker, two black American sisters are separated, one lives for decades in Africa, then returns home. In Bennett, two English sisters are separated and one lives in Paris for several decades, then rejoins her sister. What advantages does each author reap by the use of parallel plots? Show how these parallel plots make possible a comparison of the effects of different environments (nurture) on persons of the same heredity (nature). How are Celie and Nettie different because of their experience in different environments? Similar because of similar heredity?

WALKER AND HALEY: ROOTS IN AFRICA

Alice Walker's novel *The Color Purple* and Alex Haley's nonfiction book *Roots* both trace black Americans' relationships to their African origin. Compare and contrast their findings, techniques, impacts.

MALCOLM X AND WALKER: ON SOJOURN IN AFRICA

In both Walker's *The Color Purple* and Malcolm X's Autobiography, an *American Negro* goes to Africa and returns a different person to his or her native land. How has Africa changed each of them? How has religion figured in each one's sojourn in Africa? What insights do they bring or send back to America? In what ways do Walker and Malcolm X agree or disagree in their conclusions?

WALKER AND FAULKNER

The Nation magazine said that *The Color Purple* "places Walker in the company of Faulkner." Compare her novel with any William Faulkner novel (e.g., *Intruder in the Dust, The Sound and the Fury*). Perhaps you would prefer *The Sound and the Fury* because Walker has said of Faulkner's black character Dilsey that she is "an embarrassment to black people." In what respect are the two novelists similar? Different?

QUILTING IN THE COLOR PURPLE

Reread the sections in this Note on "Quilting as a **Theme** and a Technique," page 13. Show how Walker's use of letters in *The Color Purple* is a literary version of the art of quilting.

For a more ambitious study of the influence of quilting on Walker's writing, read her earlier novels, *The Third Life of Grange Copeland* and *Meridian*. Spark your own impressions by rereading the sections on "Quilting" in this Note.

WALKER: GORDIMER, PATON, CONRAD

Report on the literary methods used by novelists in their depiction of white imperialism. Compare Walker's techniques in

The Color Purple with Alan Paton's in *Cry. The Beloved Country*, and/or Joseph Conrad's in *Heart of Darkness*, and/or Nadine Gordimer's in *A Guest of Honor*, all of which deal with white oppression of blacks.

WALKER AND BEARDEN

Study the relationship of Walker's quilting technique in *The Color Purple* to Romare Bearden's collage paintings. Why is quilting such an effective device for representing the black experience in America?

WALKER'S "WOMANISM"

Read Walker's preface to her book In Search of Our Mothers' Gardens. Note that she says that "womanist is to feminist as purple is to lavender." Reread our section in this Note on "From Black Feminism to 'Womanism.'" Show how the womanist concept must have evolved as Walker worked on *The Color Purple*.

ONCE AND PURPLE

Show how Walker's poems (like "African Images") relate to the Nettie sections of *The Color Purple*.

FEMALE FRIENDSHIP AND EROTICISM

Discuss the **themes** of female friendship and woman's eroticism as variously treated in Walker's *The Color Purple*. Toni Morrison's *Sula*, and Zora Neale Hurston's *Their Eyes Were Watching God*.

BLACK ENGLISH

Reread our discussion on Black English. Contrast Walker's use of Black English with Zora Hurston's in her *Their Eyes Were Watching God*, or Toni Cade Bambara's in her short stories, or June Jordan's in her novels.

RACISM AND SEXISM: AFRICA AND THE AMERICAN SOUTH

In what ways does *The Color Purple* dramatize the white race's treatment of blacks? the complex interaction of racism and sexism in the American South? and in Africa itself? (Reread "Walker's Life, Works...")

CHARACTER PORTRAYAL IN THE COLOR PURPLE

After rereading our "Character Analysis," select one major character in *The Color Purple* and retrace his or her development as a person, e.g., how has Albert become such a "terrible person?" What web of inner and outer circumstances brings about Celie's "awakening?" In what ways is Shug a familiar figure in black culture (the blues singer) but still an individualized character?

AFRICANS AND AFRICAN-AMERICANS

What similarities does Nettie discover between the Olinkas in Africa and the black people in the American South?

DUBOYCE AND DUBOIS

Show how Walker's character DuBoyce may well be modeled on W. E. B. DuBois (1868-1963). DuBois earned a Ph.D. at Harvard, cofounded the National Association for the Advancement of Colored People, which led the civil rights demands for equality in America. Disillusioned in the United States, he took up the cause of worldwide black liberation, became a Communist, and moved to Ghana. His many books include an autobiography.

THE "BLACK MAMMY"

Show how the characterization of Sofia contradicts the smug stereotypes that whites have of "black mammies" (that no matter how they are treated, they love all white children).

SEWING AND SEXISM

Show that Celie's teaching Mister how to sew revises the concept of gender-specific work (that cooking and sewing are female tasks, running the government and sailing the seas are male tasks, and so on). How does Mister's learning a "female" task contribute toward his growth as a person? Psychology majors (and majors-to-be) might want to put this into the context of Carl Jung's theory of the animus and anima and their role in individuation.

CRITICS' RESPONSE

Report on the critics' response to *The Color Purple*, including that the most hurtful reviews were written by black men. See our chapter "Critics Respond to the Novel, *The Color Purple*'" page 82, for tips on which critics you'll be most interested in.

WALKER VERSUS BLACK MALE CRITICS

Report on Walker's response to black male critics in her article in the November 1986 *MS*.

BLACK WRITERS AS CHARACTERS IN WALKER'S FICTION

Richard Wright, African-American writer of such classics as *Native Son* and *The God that Failed*, appears as a character in Walker's short story "A Sudden Trip Home in the Spring" (1982). African-American woman writer Audre Lorde appears in Walker's story "Coming Apart" (1982). Report on Alice Walker's use of African-American writers as characters in her fiction.

For a more ambitious study of Walker's use of Wright as a character in her fiction, read a biography or a biographical article about Wright. How well does Walker's character represent the actual person?

BLACK FEMALE LITERARY TRADITION

Read Walker's essays "In Search of Our Mothers' Gardens" (1974) and "Looking for Zora" (1975). Report on Walker's exploration of the black female literary tradition.

For a more intensive study of the subject, read some of the works of Hurston discussed in "Looking for Zora."

RUKEYSER'S INFLUENCE ON WALKER

We have seen that in a suicidal mood, Alice Walker wrote many poems and stuffed them into the mailbox of Muriel Rukeyser, her writing teacher at Sarah Lawrence College and one of America's leading poets. Read Walker's book of poetry *Once* (1968) and a book of Rukeyser's poetry (published before 1968) and report on "Rukeyser's Influence on the Poet Walker." Compare them for their themes, poetic form, music, style, tone, use of metaphor.

AWAKENING THEME IN WALKER, CHOPIN, BRADBURY

Discuss the **theme** of "the awakening" in selected American novels, e.g., Walker's *The Color Purple*, Ray Bradbury's *Fahrenheit 451*, and Kate Chopin's *The Awakening*. How are the main characters awakened to the truth of the world around them; of their role in it?

PATRIARCHY AS SEEN BY FEMALE WRITERS

Discuss the patriarchal system of society as it is explored in Walker's *The Color Purple* and Chopin's *The Awakening*. Explore the mind-set of the male characters, their assumptions about women in general, the rights accorded to each sex, the "double standard."

THE NATURE OF GOD

Compare and contrast Celie's concepts of God with those of Shug, Albert, Nettie, and other characters. How do the male characters use the Bible to justify their male chauvinist attitudes? What are the reasons for and results of Celie's addressing her early letters to God?

SPIELBERG AND WALKER: FILM AND NOVEL

Watch Steven Spielberg's film version of *The Color Purple*. Explore the points made in our chapter on the film as well as the conclusions you come to yourself. How do the novel and the film compare in their treatment of Mister? Of female friendship? Of the lesbian **theme**? Of the Memphis experience? Of the African experience? Of the American South?

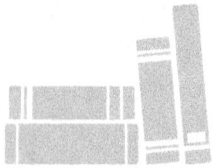

BIBLIOGRAPHY

BOOKS BY ALICE WALKER

Once: Poems. New York: Harcourt, Brace & World, 1968.

The Third Life of Grange Copeland. New York: Harcourt, Brace & Jovanovich, 1970.

In Love & Trouble: Stories of Black Women. New York: Harcourt, Brace & Jovanovich, 1973.

Revolutionary Petunias and Other Poems. New York: Harcourt, Brace & Jovanovich, 1973.

Langston Hughes, American Poet. New York: Harper & Row, 1974.

Meridian. New York: Harcourt, Brace & Jovanovich, 1976.

Good Night Willie Lee, I'll See You in the Morning. *New York: Dial, 1979.*

Ed. I Love Myself When I am Laughing: A Zora Neale Hurston Reader. *Old Westbury, New York: Feminist Press, 1979.*

You Can't Keep A Good Woman Down: Stories. New York: Harcourt, Brace & Jovanovich, 1981; London: Women's Press, 1981.

The Color Purple. New York: Harcourt, Brace & Jovanovich, 1982; London: Women's Press, 1983.

In Search of Our Mothers' Gardens: Womanist Prose. *New York: Harcourt, Brace & Jovanovich, 1983.*

Horses Make The Landscape Look More Beautiful: Poems. *New York: Harcourt, Brace & Jovanovich, 1984.*

WALKER MATERIAL ON THE COLOR PURPLE

BBC Documentary, "Alice Walker & *The Color Purple*," 1986.

"Celie's Voice," *MS.*, Vol. XIV, No. 6, December 1985, pp. 71-72, 96.

"In the Closet of the Soul," *MS.*, Vol. XV, No. 5, November 1986, pp. 32-35.

"On Making *The Color Purple*," *Sojourner*, April 1986, p. 16.

"Writing *The Color Purple*," *In Search of Our Mothers' Gardens: Womanist Prose*. New York: Harcourt, Brace & Jovanovich, 1983, pp. 356-60.

INTERVIEWS OF ALICE WALKER

O'Brien, John, *Interviews with Black Writers*. New York: Liveright, 1973, pp. 186-221.

Harris, Jessica, "Interview with Alice Walker, *Essence*, 7, July 1976.

Steinem, Gloria, "Do You Know This Woman? She Knows You-A Profile of Alice Walker," *MS.*, 10, June 1982, pp. 35-37, 89-94.

Washington, Mary Helen, "Her Mother's Gifts," *MS.*, 10, June 1982, p. 38.

Abramson, Pam, "Alice Walker Makes the Big Time with Black Folk Talk," *California Living*, August 15, 1982, pp. 16-20.

Tate, Claudia, "Alice Walker," in *Black Women Writers at Work*, ed. Tate. New York: Continuum, 1983, pp. 175-187.

Porter, Yvonne, *Colorlines: A Cultural Potpourri of the Arts*, Vol. 2, No. 3, 1983, p. 19.

Bradley, David, "Novelist Alice Walker: Telling the Black Woman's Story," *New York Times Sunday Magazine*, January 8, 1984, pp. 25-37.

Featherston, Elena, "Alice Walker on Alice Walker," *San Francisco Focus*, Vol. 32, No. 12, December 1985, p. 95.

Christian, Barbara, "A Private Conversation with Alice Walker," *American Program Bureau*, Inc., Telethon via Satellite, November 5, 1986.

SELECTED REVIEWS OF THE NOVEL THE COLOR PURPLE

"Briefly Noted," Review of *The Color Purple*, *The New Yorker*, No. 6, September 1982, p. 106.

Harris, Trudier, "On *The Color Purple*: Stereotypes and Silence," *Black American Literature Forum*, 18, (1984), pp. 155-61.

Henderson, Mae G., *The Color Purple: Revisions and Redefinitions, SAGE*, Vol. II, No. 1, Spring 1985 pp. 14-18.

Pinckney, Darryl, "Black Victims, Black Villains," *The New York Review of Books*, Vol. XXXIV, No. 1, January 29, 1987, pp. 17-20.

Porter, Yvonne, *Colorlines: A Cultural Potpourri of the Arts*, Vol. 2, No. 3, 1983, p. 20.

Prescott, Peter, "A Long Road to Liberation," Review of *The Color Purple*, *Newsweek*, No. 21, June 1985.

Tsuruta-Randall, Dorothy, "Review of *The Color Purple*," *The Black Scholar*, Vol. 14, No. 3, Summer 1983, pp. 54-55.

Smith, Barbara, "Sexual Oppression Unmasked," Review of *The Color Purple*, *Callaloo: A Black South Journal of Arts & Letters*, Vol. 7, No. 3, Fall 1984, pp. 170-176.

Smith, Dinitia, "Celie, You a Tree," Review of *The Color Purple*, *The Nation*, No. 4, September 1982, pp. 181-83.

Watkins, Mel, "Some Letters Went to God," Review of *The Color Purple*, *New York Times Book Review*, June 25, 1982, p. 7.

SELECTED REVIEWS OF THE FILM THE COLOR PURPLE

Brown, Tony, "*The Color Purple* Is White," *California Voice*, January 5, 1986.

Corsaro, Kim, "Review of *The Color Purple*," *Coming Up*, January 1986, p. 30.

Dandridge, Rita B., "In Adapting the Novel, Spielberg Left Out Too Much," *Black Film Review*, Vol. 2, No. 2, Spring 1986, pp. 17, 20, 26.

Forbes, Calvin, "Searching the Ideology of Meaning," *Black Film Review*, Vol. 2, No. 2, Spring 1986, pp. 17, 20, 28.

Halprin, Sara, "*The Color Purple*: Community of Women," *Jumpcut: A Review of Contemporary Media*, No. 31, pp. 1, 28.

Hamlin, Willie T., M.D., "*The Color Purple*: Apartheid's Orgy of Black Male Hatred," *Oakland Post*, January 15, 1986, pp. 4, 12.

Jaehne, Karen, "The Final Word," *Cineaste*, Vol. XV, No. 1, 1986.

Muhammad, Abdul Wali, "Purple Poison Pulses Through Community," *The Final Call*, Vol.5, No. 6, January 27, 1986, pp. 4-6.

Nicholsen, David, "From Coast to Coast 'Purple' Aroused Passions," *Black Film Review*, Vol. 2, No. 2, Spring 1986, pp. 18-19.

Pinckney, Darryl, "Black Victims, Black Villains," *The New York Review of Books*, Vol. XXXIV, No. 1, January 29, 1987, pp. 17-20.

Raymond, Monica, "*The Color Purple*: Celluloid Slickness," *Sojourner*, February 1986, p. 32.

Taylor, Robert, "Spielberg Paints a Vibrant 'Purple'," *Oakland Tribune*, December 19, 1985, Section E, pp. 1, 4.

Teish, Luisa, "Pro Color Purple," *Daily Californian Black History Month Special*, February 11, 1986, pp. 8, 14.

Walter, Earl Jr., "One Man's View," *Black Film Review*, Vol. 2, No. 2, Spring 1986, pp. 16, 19.

Wilson, Marti, "A Disappointment But We Still Have the Book," *Black Film Review*, Spring 1986, pp. 17, 20, 26.

Wilson, Marti, "Taking the Color Out of 'Purple'," *Sojourner*, February 1986, pp. 32, 33.

REFERENCES ON ALICE WALKER'S WORKS

Babb, Valerie, "*The Color Purple*: Writing to Undo What Writing Has Done," *Phylon: The Atlanta University Review of Race and Culture*, Vol. XLVII, No. 2, Summer 1986, pp. 107-116.

Christian, Barbara, "Alice Walker, The Black Woman Writer as Wayward," *Black Women Writers, 1950-1980*, Mari Evans, ed. Garden City: Doubleday, 1984, pp. 457-77.

____, "Alice Walker, A Literary Biography," *Dictionary of Literary Biography*, Vol. 33: African-American Fiction Writers After 1955, Thadius Davis & Trudier Harris, ed. Detroit: Gale Research Company, 1984, pp. 257-70.

____, "An Angle of Seeing: Motherhood in Buchi Emecheta's The Joys of Motherhood and Alice Walker's Meridian," *Black Feminist Criticism: Perspectives on Black Women Writers*. New York: Pergamon Press, 1985, pp. 211-248.

____, "The Contrary Black Women of Alice Walker: A Study of Female **Protagonists** in In Love & Trouble," *Black Scholar*, No. 12, March, April, 1981, pp. 21-30, 70-71.

____, "No More Buried Lives: The **Theme** of Lesbianism in Audre Lorde's Zami, Gloria Naylor's The Women of Brewster Place, Ntozake Shange's Sassafras, Cypress and Indigo and Alice Walker's *The Color Purple*," *Black Feminist Criticism: Perspectives on Black Women Writers*. New York: Pergamon, 1985, pp. 187-204.

_____, "Novels for Everyday Use," *Black Women Novelists: The Development of A Tradition, 1892-1976*. Westport, Conn.: Greenwood Press, 1980, pp. 180-238.

_____, "We Are the Ones That We Have Been Waiting For: Political Content in Alice Walker's Novels," *Women's Studies International Forum*, Vol. 9, No. 4, Winter 1986, pp. 421-426.

Dworkin, Susan, "*The Color Purple* Becomes A Movie," *MS.*, Vol. XIV, No. 6, December 1985, pp. 66-70, 94-95.

Erickson, Peter, "Cast Out Alone/ To Heal/ and Re-create/ Ourselves: Family Based Identity in the Work of Alice Walker," *CLA Journal*, No. 23, September 1979, pp. 71-94.

Fifes, Elizabeth, "Alice Walker, The Dialect & Letters of *The Color Purple*," *Contemporary American Women Writing: Narrative Strategies, Rainwater and Schweick*, ed. Lexington: University of Kentucky Press, 1986, pp. 155-65.

Freeman, Alma, "Zora Neale Hurston and Alice Walker: A Spiritual Kinship," *Sage: A Scholarly Journal on Black Women*, Vol. II, No. 1, Spring 1985, pp. 37-40.

Gaston, Karen C., "Women in the Lives of Grange Copeland," *CLA Journal*, No. 24, March, 1981, pp. 276-286.

Harris, Trudier, "Folklore in the Fiction of Alice Walker: A Perpetuation of Historical and Literary Traditions," *Black American Literature Forum*, No. 2, Spring 1977, pp.3-8.

_____, "Violence in The Third Life of Grange Copeland," *CLA Journal*, No. 19, December 1975, pp. 238-247.

McDowell, Deborah, "The Changing Same: Generational Connections and Black Women Novelists," *New Literary History*, Vol. 18, No. 2, Winter 1987, pp. 281-302.

____, "The Self in Bloom: Alice Walker's Meridian," *CLA Journal*, No. 24, March 1981, pp. 262-275.

Parker-Smith, Bettye J., "Alice Walker's Women: In Search of Peace of Mind," *Black Women Writers 1950-80*, Mari Evans, ed. Garden City: Doubleday, 1984, pp.478-493.

Pryse, Marjorie, "Zora Neale Hurston, Alice Walker and the 'Ancient Power' of Black Women," *Conjuring: Black Women, Fiction and Literary Tradition, Marjorie Pryse and Hortense J. Spillers*, eds. Bloomington: Indiana University Press, 1985, pp. 1-23.

Royster, Phillip M., "In Search of Our Fathers' Arms: Alice Walker's Persona of the Alienated Darling," *Black American Literature Forum*, Vol. 20, No. 4, Winter 1986, pp.348-371.

Sadoff, Dianne F., "Black Matrilineage: The Case of Alice Walker and Zora Neale Hurston," *Signs*, Vol. 11, No. 2, Autumn 1985, pp. 4-26.

Washington, Mary Helen, "An Essay on Alice Walker," *Sturdy Black Bridges*, Roseann Bell, Bettye Parker and Beverly Guy-Sheftall, eds. New York: Anchor Press/Doubleday, 1979, pp. 133-49.

Watkins, Mel, "Sexism, Racism & Black Women Writers," *The New York Review of Books*, June 15, 1986, pp. 1, 35-37.

Willis, Susan, "Alice Walker's Women," *Specifying: Black Women Writing the American Experience*. Madison, Wis.: The University of Wisconsin Press, 1987, pp. 110-128.

EXPLORE THE ENTIRE LIBRARY OF BRIGHT NOTES STUDY GUIDES

From Shakespeare to Sinclair Lewis and from Plato to Pearl S. Buck, The Bright Notes Study Guide library spans hundreds of volumes, providing clear and comprehensive insights into the world's greatest literature. Discover more, faster with the Bright Notes Study Guide to the classics you're reading today.

See the entire library of available Bright Notes guides at **BrightNotes.com**

Available in print and digital wherever books are sold

IP INFLUENCE PUBLISHERS

www.ingramcontent.com/pod-product-compliance
Lightning Source LLC
LaVergne TN
LVHW012058070526
838200LV00070BA/2867